HOW TO STRENGTHEN YOUR FAITH

ANDREW MURRAY

 *Whitaker House*

All Scripture quotations are from the *King James Version* (KJV) of the Bible.

HOW TO STRENGTHEN YOUR FAITH

ISBN: 0-88368-128-5
Printed in the United States of America
Copyright © 1997 by Whitaker House

Whitaker House
30 Hunt Valley Circle
New Kensington, PA 15068

1 2 3 4 5 6 7 8 9 10 11 12 / 06 05 04 03 02 01 00 99 98 97

Contents

1. The Necessity of True Faith 7

2. By the Spirit and the Word 13

3. Reaching Out for the Gift of Faith 23

4. Faith and Repentance 29

5. Becoming a Child of God 39

6. Humility and Penitence 49

7. The Certainty of Faith 57

8. The Surrender of Faith 63

9. Receiving and Nourishing Faith 73

10. Justification: By Faith or by Works? 85

11. Faith That Glorifies God 91

12. Expressions of Faith 101

Chapter 1

The Necessity of True Faith

He that believeth and is baptized shall
be saved; but he that believeth not
shall be damned.
—Mark 16:16

I f you have decided to seek your own salvation, and not the salvation that Christ has offered to you, this passage of Scripture is for you: *"He that believeth...shall be saved."* God does not require anything more than simple faith. However, He will not settle for anything less. Faith is the only way to salvation; there is no other way. *"He that believeth not shall be damned."* Thus, God seeks to bring us to faith in Christ by the attractions and charms of His grace on the one hand, and by the threat of His wrath on the other. Faith is the one indispensable prerequisite of salvation.

No matter how much people may be opposed to this method, the time will come when both the lost in hell and the saved in heaven will justify God in His ways. The whole universe will acknowledge the

7

equity of this sentence: *"He that believeth not shall be damned."* Our gracious Lord has always met the sinner with the wonderful offer of complete forgiveness, and He bestows on him all that is necessary for an everlasting salvation. He requires no worthiness or merit, but simply this: man should accept what is offered to him and believe what has been said to him.

In order to remove every hindrance to faith and to win people's hearts, God ordained the glad tidings of salvation to be sent through His own Son, Jesus Christ, who manifested Himself in the most loving and attractive form. He also sealed His love with His own precious blood. As a result, he who still does not believe *"shall be damned."* When a man will not allow himself to be redeemed from all his former sins, he sets the seal upon them all over again. To his former sins, he adds the greatest sins of all: he has affronted God's authority, despised God's love, lightly esteemed God's Son, defied God's vengeance, and thrust God's salvation away from him. Through his unbelief, he shows his enmity against God and his rejection of God. Therefore, the decree cannot, and may not, be put forth in any other way but *"he that believeth not shall be damned."*

The absolute necessity of faith is no less confirmed when we study the other side of this verse: *"He that believeth...shall be saved."* Man has nothing, absolutely nothing, of his own to contribute to the attainment of salvation. He cannot put himself in any position that will speed him along to it. And yet, the Lord will do nothing but reign over a willing people. Man is not a stone; he must do his part. How can this be, that man can do nothing and yet should do something? It is faith that solves this difficult enigma.

Faith is manifested in the acknowledgment of poverty and misery, in the confession of inability and helplessness. Faith is seen in consent, submission, and surrender to the grace of God, which is to be everything in us. God cannot require more than faith, and He cannot require less, for He will not do any injustice to His own honor or to the freedom of man. He requires faith, faith alone, and His grace bends down low to our weakness. *"He that believeth...shall be saved."*

Notice that there are two alternatives: to believe and be saved, or to be unbelieving and therefore damned. Make your choice. Do not think about it any longer or ask if there is no other way. Rather, come, submit yourself to God and to the word of His grace: *"He that believeth...shall be saved."* Put aside the secret thought that something else may, after all, still be necessary.

You may feel that everlasting salvation is too great a blessing for the meager and paltry faith that you have. You may also find it too hazardous for you, in your sinfulness, to venture so far merely upon faith. Yet, it is God who has spoken, and He grants salvation only to those who come to Him by faith. He who possesses this faith has everything, for by it he has Christ. He who does not possess faith has nothing, even if he possesses everything else. Faith is absolutely necessary.

A GLORIOUS PORTRAYAL OF JESUS

Study the verse once again: *"He that believeth...shall be saved; but he that believeth not shall be damned."* In Mark's gospel, we find the story of a woman who believed and was saved. *"For she said, If I may touch but his clothes, I shall be whole"* (Mark 5:28). What a glorious portrayal of the Lord Jesus is given by this woman's simple words! She regarded Him as so filled with the divine power of life—as He most certainly is—that it flowed out to everyone who even touched Him in faith. She felt assured that even the slightest fellowship with Him would be blessed and that she would experience the healing power of the life that was in Him.

She did not doubt either His power or His willingness, even for a moment. Had He not come for the sick? Then why should she continue to beg, as if she had no claim to His healing? No, she knew that there is healing in Him and that this healing was also for her. She would have doubted her right to make use of the light of the sun sooner than her right to Jesus. She would have questioned whether she could take a drink of water from a rushing river sooner than nurture the thought that there was no health for her to be found with Jesus.

Oh, doubting soul, I pray that you would think of the Lord Jesus just as this woman thought of Him. It is always the good pleasure of the Father that all fullness should dwell in Him (Col. 1:19). The Father has purposely made all the fullness of His love and His life to dwell in Jesus, the Son of Man, so that it may be truly visible and accessible to us. In Him dwells the power of a new and holy life from the dead, which He obtained by making atonement for our sins. This new life has the power to impart health to souls who are sick unto death. It is the life intended for us sinful, dead, condemned sinners.

The Necessity of True Faith

I urge you to understand what the woman shows you by her example. The blessing and the approval of Jesus are the seal of the truth of her words. In Jesus is life, life even for the most wretched sinner.

A PICTURE OF TRUE FAITH

The story of this woman is not only a glorious portrayal of Jesus Christ, but it is also a marvelous picture of true faith as our means of participating in the fullness of Jesus. The woman knew that she had no work to do, no great strength to put forth, to receive her healing. She had no need to consider, as she might have done with other doctors or healers, whether she was really in a position to pay the fees that would be demanded. No, she merely had to touch Him, that is, she merely had to take possession of what was already prepared for her. The healing was there as soon as she stretched out her hand to receive it.

Anxious soul, you have already sought for too long to make yourself fit for the great work of believing. Therefore, put an end to this fruitless preparation, and let this poor woman's example help to cure you of your error. Everything is ready in Jesus; you merely have to stretch out your hand. He is given to you by the Father and stands ready for your deliverance. All you have to do is to touch Him with the firm conviction of faith: "Jesus is for me."

Reach out with the simple thought, "I have a right to Him; in Him there is deliverance for me also." Touch Him, and, as truly as His name is Jesus, you will be delivered. You might not immediately feel this deliverance, but just wait, hold on, and

11

say from day to day, "If I touch Him, I will be made whole." You will then become conscious of this healing.

A DEPICTION OF GREATER BLESSINGS

The story of this woman also provides a beautiful depiction of even greater blessings that Jesus gives to faith. That the woman was healed was a great blessing in itself. However, the Scripture speaks of an even richer blessing—that Jesus observed her, the poor, trembling believer who would not have hidden herself in shame, even if others were seeking Him in the crowd. He gave her the assurance of His good pleasure and His favor. He caused her to confess Him openly. He praised her faith and thus made her an example and a blessing for thousands.

If you are looking and yearning for the salvation of your soul, try to understand what is awaiting you with Jesus, and what you may hope for from Him. Not only will He make you a partaker of forgiveness of sins and deliverance from destruction, but the friendship and love of the Savior will also be your portion. By these, He will make you a blessing to others. Beloved reader, what more is needed to bring you to say humbly and with faltering lips, following this woman's example, *"If I may touch but his clothes, I shall be whole"* (Mark 5:28)? When you reach out for Him, you will find that He is the source of true faith.

Chapter 2

By the Spirit
and the Word

*So then faith cometh by hearing,
and hearing by the word of God.*
—Romans 10:17

The Scriptures exhort us to faith dozens upon dozens of times, and, almost as many times, they speak of faith as an act of man. However, it is only in a few instances that it is specifically said that faith is the work of the Spirit. Thus, when we insist on faith as a work in which man must be active and in which he must trustfully and perseveringly use some kind of helpful means, it sometimes appears as if we forget who the Author of faith is. This, however, is by no means the case.

THE SPIRIT WORKING IN YOU

Those who are the most eager to follow the exhortations in the Scriptures will also be the ones who most deeply feel the truth about man's complete dependence on the Spirit as the Spirit of faith.

Anyone who knows that there is a Spirit to bestow faith, also knows that he may strive to exercise that faith with zeal and with hope.

The proper understanding of this truth is of great importance for anxious souls. They must especially know that, when they wait for the influence of the Spirit to carry them on to faith, they must not expect this influence to be unveiled to them in a conscious and tangible manner. The beginnings of life are hidden in darkness. In other words, the first workings of the Spirit are not known or observed. The sinner must work on, although he is not conscious that the Spirit is at work within. He must be as ready in the darkness as he is in the daylight. In his own strength, the sinner must be ready to obey and to strive to believe.

The sinner must also have a great confidence that the Spirit will work in him through the Word. He must hold fast, expecting that the Spirit will be recognized sooner or later as the power that has put him in a position to believe. This faith will then be the first sure sign that the changed sinner now has the Spirit, who is always the Spirit of faith.

Faith is the Spirit's eternal manifestation, the form in which He reveals Himself and by which He becomes known. It cannot be, "Once I have the Spirit, then I will believe." Rather, it must be, "When I believe, then I will know that the Spirit has caused this result in me."

In this way, one who seeks to know that he has the Spirit of faith may have his desire fully gratified. He will learn that there is something more in him than mere faith, that faith is not his own work. He will learn that the Divine Creator of the new life is

14

in him. As the sinner trustfully and unreservedly
surrenders to live through faith, the Spirit will witness with his spirit that, after we believe, we are
sealed with the Spirit. *"Ye know him; for he dwelleth
with you, and shall be in you"* (John 14:17).

STIRRED UP TO MORE FAITH

By His divine, indwelling power, the Holy Spirit
always stirs up in the soul more and more faith, car-
rying a believer into all the riches of the promises of
God. When the believer is active in faith according to
the Word of God, the Spirit gives him confidence to
lay hold of every blessing.

Thus, the one influence always operates upon
the other: the more fully a man believes, the clearer
the revelation of the Spirit becomes. The more fully
the Spirit works in a man's soul, the more he grows
in the life of faith and confidence. And, at length,
but not in the way that most of us would picture for
ourselves, he comes to experience the blessedness of
which I write—of having the Spirit of faith.

Seeker of salvation, why do you not believe? The
Spirit of God is a Spirit of faith. It is the Spirit of
God who has broken your slumber and made you
anxious to believe. It is the Spirit who will help you
in the conflict for faith, in which you think you are
abandoned by Him. He is given in answer to your
prayers. Let the thought encourage you, that where
there is someone who desires salvation, the Spirit
will certainly work faith in him.

At the outset, you are not yet in a position to
recognize His working. You are not yet accustomed
to His ways; His methods are still unknown to you.

Yet, although He is hidden, He is working in you. Therefore, rely on His operation. He is the Spirit who unconsciously draws and strengthens the one who desires to believe. Believe, then, for the Spirit will give you faith. Work, then, *"for it is God which worketh in you"* (Phil. 2:13).

When you have believed and have come to know Him as the Spirit of faith, you must then be faithful to Him. Yield yourself wholly to Him; open your heart entirely for Him. Through Him, let there be a progress *"from faith to faith"* (Rom. 1:17), until, with full certainty, you are able to witness this truth: *"We having the same spirit of faith,...therefore...we also believe"* (2 Cor. 4:13).

THE SPIRIT WORKS BY THE WORD

Here is the simple answer to the question, "How does faith arise in the soul?" The Spirit, the Author of faith, uses a means to achieve this purpose, and that means is the Word. It cannot be otherwise.

The Spirit can only do His work in man by using the natural gifts that remained in him after the Fall. Through His supernatural power, the Holy Spirit renews and sanctifies those gifts. He bends the will of a man by awakening desire in him. He works upon his emotions by presenting the loveliness of Jesus. And, when He works faith in the man's soul, He presents the truth in order to thereby awaken confidence.

I take it for granted that you, my reader, are one who has been awakened. I assume that you, desiring to be saved, are looking for rescue. You long to be freed from your sin, and so you ask, "How do I come

to faith in Jesus?" The answer is, "By the Word."
"But, what am I to do with the Word?" Do with it
what you would do with any ordinary message that
you cannot believe at once.

Suppose that tidings are brought to you of a
great inheritance that comes to you. You had not
been expecting it and cannot believe that such great
happiness and wealth are now yours. What will you
do? You will ask if the messenger is trustworthy.
Then, if you are sure that you can trust his message,
you will ask him again and again if you are indeed
the person intended, in order to be absolutely certain. Or, if he has brought a letter of conveyance or a
will, you will read it repeatedly. And thus, by expla-
nation and confirmation of his message, you will become convinced and will believe. Faith comes by
trusting someone's word.

It is likewise in divine things. When the message
comes to you, saying, "Jesus is a Savior for sinners,
also for you," do you ask if you are to believe Him
who speaks? You ask, and the answer is, "Yes, for He
is the true God." Do you ask if there has been a mis-
understanding or if you are really the person intended? You ask, and again the answer is, "Yes, for
the message is to every sinner."

LISTEN TO THE MESSAGE

After that, it becomes your duty to earnestly listen to the message. You must ask repeatedly, un-
ceasingly—for the matter is of great importance—
"Will I or will I not believe?" And, the more you simply take the Word, read and read again the message
of God, and contemplate one promise after another

17

with which God has made sure that the Savior is for every sinner, the sooner you will feel constrained to say, "It is true. God says it; therefore, I must believe it." The Spirit will have ministered the truth of the Word to your soul.

O poor sinner, cease asking what your own heart feels, as one who wants to be saved. Stop looking for the basis of faith in yourself. Listen now to what the Spirit says through the Word: Jesus is the Savior of sinners. Listen to it again and again. Let your soul become occupied the whole day with the thought, "God says it; therefore, it must be so." And, continue with this, no matter how wretched and dark the condition of your heart may be. Ask simply from day to day, "What does the Word say?" Take and carry that Word in your heart, and you will speedily experience that *"faith cometh by...the word."*

This activity will be far from making you think that faith is a work of your own power. Instead, you will acknowledge that the Spirit works by the Word. Remember, faith arises in the soul as the Holy Spirit instills the Word in your heart. Your use of the Word will give you cause, as well as the right, to hope for His help. You will experience how faith is not merely a reasoning of the intellect. And, at the same time, you will know how faithful God is to bestow His grace on this means of faith. With His blessing He will crown the soul who honors His Word.

THE WORD IS A SEED

The Holy Spirit brings the Word of God to our hearts, and our faith grows from the seeds of the

Scripture that He instills in us. Then, through the Spirit and the Word, our faith produces fruit that is pleasing to God. In Luke 8:11, we find a wonderful picture of how the Word of God causes our faith to be fruitful: *"Now the parable is this: the seed is the word of God."*

The Word is set forth very simply and strikingly in this parable. The cold, dead earth can bring forth nothing of itself but thorns and thistles. It does not have the power to give man nutritious corn. However, when a farmer desires to have that corn, he takes good seed and plants it in the ground that had until then brought forth nothing but weeds.

The soil receives the seed and keeps it in the dark secrecy and silence of the ground. Encouraged by the sunshine and moistened by the dew of heaven, it begins to grow. Thus, the cold, dead earth gradually becomes the mother of a beautiful crop. The life is not in the earth, but in the seed. And yet, the earth is just as essential as the living seed before the harvest can be reaped.

Although the seed does not receive life from the earth, the seed cannot yield its fruit without the earth having its share in the work. The earth offers the seed its soil, in which the root begins to grow. The seed is then kept in the ground until it is ready to make an appearance as a plant above ground.

This is a glorious and instructive picture of the new life of grace. Like the seed, the Word has a divine, life-giving power. Like the earth, the heart has no life in itself and can produce no good fruit of itself. Like the seed that is sown in the earth, the Word is sown in the heart and committed to it, simply to be received and kept there. God has lodged in the seed a living power that ensures that the ground—although in and of itself it is wholly incapable of bringing forth anything but weeds—will be changed into a fruitful field.

Thus, no matter how helpless you may feel yourself to be, the living seed of God's Word will send forth its roots in your heart and, sprouting upward, bring forth fruit. Sinner, yearning for salvation, all you have to do is to acknowledge that a living power is presented to you in every word of God. And then, relying on this truth, you must keep the Word of God in your heart. The certainty of fruit does not depend on any ability of yours, but on the faithfulness of God. Your only duty is, by prayerful consideration and faithful keeping of God's Word, to prepare a place for the fruit in your heart. Then the Spirit will ensure that the seeds grow to produce that fruit.

A FRUITFUL FAITH

Do not mourn any longer, then, that your heart is so hard and so full of weeds. Instead, understand what you see every day—that by keeping the seed that the Spirit has planted, the dead earth is transformed into a fruitful field. Faith is not present in you before you receive the Word. Nevertheless, life is in the Word, and it is by the Word that faith is first awakened.

Meanwhile, do not forget that there are many kinds of seed, and every kind bears fruit according to its nature. Suppose, for example, that a child of God has encountered adversity and longs for comfort. He chooses one of the promises of God to His people, sows it in his heart, and keeps it there. The desired fruit, God's comfort, then emerges.

Similarly, if you are troubled about your sins, you need to have the promises of God's grace in relation to the ungodly. The Holy Spirit will show you seeds of Scripture according to your need. *"The LORD is gracious and full of compassion"* (Ps. 111:4). *"He will abundantly pardon"* (Isa. 55:7). *"Him that cometh to me I will in no wise cast out"* (John 6:37). *"Christ died for the ungodly"* (Rom. 5:6). That is the kind of seed you must use.

Every one of these verses is a heavenly grain of seed containing power for eternal life. Every one of them, when it begins to sprout, is sufficient to bring forth the fruits of faith and peace and life. If even one of them is faithfully kept in the heart, faith will be born of it automatically.

Life is in the seed. The seed of God's Word has the divine power of life. Therefore, take the heavenly seed, let the Holy Spirit place it in your heart, and keep it there. Although you do not actually feel that you believe, resolve at least to hold firm to the thought: "It is the living Word of God. God will give the increase in His own time." (See 1 Corinthians 3:6.)

A seed needs time for development and growth. It must be kept a long time quietly beneath the ground, but one day it begins to sprout. Therefore, continue daily to fill your heart with the Word of promise and of grace. The true God, the Holy Spirit, and His living Word are the guarantees that your experience will be according to this verse: *"Faith cometh by hearing, and hearing by the word of God."*

Chapter 3

Reaching Out for the
Gift of Faith

Unto you it is given in the behalf
of Christ...to believe on him.
—Philippians 1:29

aith is a gift of God. This truth has often been
the cause of fear and dread, yet it should not be
so. It should yield reasons for gladness and
hope. It is a perverse overstatement to say, "Faith is
a gift, and so I do not know if I will ever receive it. If
it were found by personal effort, and if I had to call it
into existence by my own power, I would then indeed
make sure that I did not remain without faith."
Many people think this way. However, the opposite
is the truth.

If you could believe of yourself, by personal effort and work, you would never be able to do it; you
would certainly be lost. But, since faith is given to
us, since there is a Lord in heaven who will implant
and cherish and care for that faith in us, then there
is hope that we may obtain and preserve it. This is a
message of joyful hope.

How to Strengthen Your Faith

FAITH GIVEN BY GRACE

The encouragement of this message of faith is made still greater in that this faith is given by grace. *"For by grace are ye saved through faith; and that not of yourselves: it is the gift of God"* (Eph. 2:8). There is no question of worthiness or merit, of wisdom or piety, of strength or dignity. Rather, faith is given to the unworthy and the ungodly. To those who do not seek Him, the sovereign God comes with His drawing grace. Through the Spirit, He brings about the conviction of sin and of the need for His love.

By His Word, God sets Jesus before all mankind as His desirable and suitable gift to the sinner, freely offered and acceptable, until you, under the hidden and effectual working of the Spirit, find confidence to take the Savior entirely to yourself. Yes, from beginning to end, along the whole way, in the midst of continual sinfulness and unfaithfulness on your part, by grace you are given the power to believe in Him.

WORKING TOWARD FAITH

The fact that faith comes by means of some effort on our part does not make it any less of a gift. Almost every gift of God comes through our own effort or by some other means. We get bread by the sweat of our brow, and yet we pray: *"Give us this day our daily bread"* (Matt. 6:11). We keep ourselves healthy with a proper diet, and yet we always thank the Lord for preserving us from sickness and death. Indeed, our having to work for faith only shows us how loving the gift is. It shows how the Lord will move and open the spirit of man when he works to take hold entirely for himself what his God will give to him.

This certainly should not deter us from working for faith. Instead, it should give us the right desire and the right spirit in which to work. The believer learns to understand that the Lord who gives the Word will also give the faith to receive it. He who has given the promise will also bestow the fulfillment. Set yourself to believe, in joyful confidence, that it is given.

LOOK TO GOD FOR FAITH

Reader, belief in Jesus is given by grace, *"for by grace are ye saved through faith"* (Eph. 2:8). Humbly ask for this grace from the Lord; wait for it at His feet in a childlike spirit. Let every experience of failure, of unbelief, of imperceptiveness, convince you of how unfortunate it would be if you had to believe out of your own strength. Learn how blessed it is that you may look to God for it. Keep yourself occupied with the Word of promise, and look to Jesus as appointed for you by God, so that you may believe in Him.

In every endeavor to take hold of Christ and the promises of grace, work in silent gladness, inspired by this Scripture: *"The promise by faith of Jesus Christ might be given to them that believe"* (Gal. 3:22). The God who has offered Jesus to you, who has awakened in you the first desire for Him, will also give you the grace to believe. In that blessed confidence, you will go forward until, secretly and gradually, faith becomes living and visible in you. Yes, thank God that *"unto you it is given...to believe on him."*

THE HAND OF FAITH

One of the most common mistakes that keeps people away from faith is that they do not feel the strength for faith. They desire first to feel faith living in them, and then they will believe. However, the command to believe comes to them while they still feel unprepared for it, while they still are not ready to believe. This they do not understand. They do not understand, because they have not observed, that readiness and ability for any work is not given before the work but only through the work. Thus, strength for faith comes after we begin to work.

When a child learns to run, he begins to learn before he can really do it, and he learns in the midst of his effort. When a man wishes to learn how to swim, he goes into the water while he cannot yet swim, because he knows that once he begins he will learn to do it in time. This law of nature has an even more glorious application in grace. God gives us commands for which we previously have no power, yet He requires obedience to them. He has every right to do so. He has told us that when we submit and set ourselves toward obedience, strength will be given when we begin. This is the spirit in which we are to believe.

Under the conviction of his unbelief, the sinner must still set himself to believe. In the assurance that power will be bestowed, he is still to make a beginning: "Lord, I believe." In this action, he must persevere and go forward.

Reaching Out for the Gift of Faith

Both aspects of this truth are very strikingly illustrated for us by the case of the man with the withered hand. Jesus *"said to the man which had the withered hand,...Stretch forth thy hand. And he did so: and his hand was restored"* (Luke 6:8, 10). He felt no power in his hand, and yet Jesus said to him, *"Stretch forth thy hand."* He saw in the Savior enough to convince him that Jesus would not mock him, that He who gave this command would certainly never issue it without giving power at the same time to carry it out. The man obeyed, and his hand was healed.

Recall the story of the woman who knew that she would be healed if she touched the hem of Jesus' garment. All she had to do was reach out for Him, and her healing came as soon as she stretched out her hand to receive it. You, likewise, simply have to stretch out your hand in order to receive all that waits for you in Christ.

REACH OUT FOR HIM

Anxious soul, the Lord Jesus who calls to you, "Believe in Me as your Savior," knows your helplessness. He speaks to you in order to rescue you from it. With a voice of power, He commands you, "Believe in Me, that I am given by God to be your Savior. Stretch out your hand to lay hold of Me and to take Me for yourself."

Listen to Him; be willing to obey Him. Remember that with the command He also gives the strength. Although you do not yet feel the power, begin; although you can still do nothing, say, as Martha did, *"I believe that thou art the Christ, the Son of*

God" (John 11:27). Show that it is your desire to believe and that you are indeed earnest about it. Know in your heart that He really speaks to you, and hear how kind and encouraging His voice is. He says to you, "Oh, unbelieving one, believe in Me." As the man with the withered hand obtained power to stretch it out at the command of Jesus, so will it be with you. Faith is God's gift to you, and all you have to do is to reach out for it.

The command, "Believe," will no longer oppress you with the thought, "I cannot do it." Instead, it will encourage you to be confident enough to say, "Jesus commands it, thus it is to be, thus it may be." And, when you have any inclination to be discouraged, if you look to Jesus and hear how cheeringly He calls to you, "You may, you must, you can believe in Me," your soul will be strengthened with an ever-growing steadfastness to entrust yourself to Him. In the endeavor to believe, strength for it is given and exercised. The hand of faith will soon be entirely healed.

You who are struggling for faith, Jesus asks you, "If I speak the truth to you, why do you not believe?" (John 8:46). He tells you the divine truth that He has come for you. He tells you the truth so that your faith may be awakened by it. I entreat you to understand this. See Him who speaks: it is Jesus, the faithful and almighty Lover. Hear His voice and do not be unbelieving any longer.

Chapter 4

Faith and Repentance

Repent ye, and believe the gospel.
—Mark 1:15

This verse of Scripture, from the beginning of Christ's preaching, contains the summary of God's will for our salvation. God desires that we repent and believe. Without repentance, there is no real faith; without faith, there is no true repentance.

Read the first part of that sentence again: without repentance, there is no real faith. God's entire purpose in sending Christ, His great purpose in giving us salvation through faith, is to win our hearts back from sin and to make them free from sin. A real desire for this salvation can obviously never arise in the heart that is not also loosed from sin and prepared to abandon it.

Faith is a surrender of the soul to God. This is an impossibility for the person who still continues to give himself to sin. Faith is taking hold of and receiving the grace of God into one's heart. It is an absurdity to

29

suppose that this can take place without a simultaneous repentance, an abandonment and casting out of sin.

Without faith, also, there is no true repentance. Repentance is not only a turning away from sin, which by itself would lead to self-righteousness, but it is also a turning back to God. This can take place only through faith. Repentance is not a work of one's own power, but a consenting, a cooperation with God's plan in God's strength. It is a trustful surrender to the redeeming grace of God. And, this can be done only through faith.

Repentance is not an actual victory over sin. Rather, the sinner has to bring every sin to the feet of the Lord Jesus, the great Victor over sin, so that He may take it away. This cannot take place unless the sinner has acknowledged, by faith, that Jesus is faithful to forgive sin and *"to cleanse us from all unrighteousness"* (1 John 1:9).

Thus, the power of repentance is faith. The more we trust that Jesus makes us free from sin, the stronger we are to turn away from it. The power of faith, on the other hand, is also repentance. The more eager to be freed from sin it causes us to be, the more dependent we are upon faith. *"Repent ye, and believe."* Anyone who observes and holds fast to both of these truths will be saved.

A CONTINUAL REPENTANCE

Faith and repentance, however, must accompany one another not only at the beginning of the way, but also on to the very end. If faith is cultivated in a one-sided fashion—without a growing repentance

of sin and the sanctification of the whole heart—
then it becomes a work merely of the mind or the
emotions. And, if repentance and sanctification
alone occupy the daily walk—without the increase of
a living faith by the promise of God's grace—such a
repentance will also lose its worth.

"Repent ye, and believe." Notice what Jesus calls
you to. Every wish and effort you make toward repentance, every remembrance of the sin that is in
you and of which you want to be free, must be a
summons to believe in Jesus. You are called to wage
war against every sin and to renounce it at His feet
with your faith set on Him. Let every thought of
faith be an encouragement to fight more bravely
against sin until your whole soul is filled with the
faith of which it is written, *"This is the victory that
overcometh the world, even our faith"* (1 John 5:4).

Thus, repentance and faith will become entirely
one in due time. *"What therefore God hath joined
together, let not man put asunder"* (Matt. 19:6). The
outgoing of your soul to Jesus will lead you away
from sin, and the simple enjoyment of His love by
faith will drive away the darkness. Then, believing
and working will no longer be incompatible. Rather,
you will know that a continually renewed faith is the
fruit of repentance, and you will continue in faith by
the strength of Jesus. Through your continued repentance, you will find the courage to persevere in
faith, the certainty of a full assurance, and the evidence before God that you are walking in faith.

Soul, why do you not believe? Do not let it be
because you will not repent. It should not be that
you are not willing to renounce sin. Do not allow
yourself to desire first to repent and then, later on,

How to Strengthen Your Faith

to believe. No, let both repentance and faith go together from this moment on: *"Repent ye, and believe."*

BEING SINCERE BEFORE GOD

In your repentance, you must also be sincere. You must allow yourself to fall before the Lord in perfect sincerity, saying, *"I believe; help thou mine unbelief"* (Mark 9:24). This is actually the most sincere thing you can do.

The Word of God attaches great value to sincerity. As a result, the desire to be sincere in one's faith is entirely justifiable. However, both experience and the consistent testimony of the Word of God show that fear and unrest also arise from this desire. How can fear and unrest arise from the desire to be sincere? There are well-founded reasons for this, as we can see from the following verse: *"The heart is deceitful above all things, and desperately wicked: who can know it?"* (Jer. 17:9).

Frequently, great mistakes are made with respect to what true sincerity is and the means by which it is obtained and increased. Many people think that sincerity is a distinct feeling that they have surrendered themselves to the Lord with a strong faith and a fervent love. This is by no means what the Word of God intends by sincerity. Sincerity is an attitude of the soul, by virtue of which we present ourselves to the Lord just as we are, neither better nor worse. A man who makes himself out to be something other than what he really is or feels is insincere. He is a man who cannot truly repent of his sin.

Faith and Repentance

It is on this basis that the words of the father of the possessed child are such a glorious example of sincerity: *"I believe; help thou mine unbelief"* (Mark 9:24). This man wished to believe, but felt that unbelief was still too strong within him. What, then, was he to do? He presented himself to the Lord just as he was. He knew that his desire was to trust in Jesus. However, he did not know if there was more unbelief than faith in his heart.

What should he have done? Should he have mourned over the unbelief that was still in him? Or, should he have just waited until he felt that he believed well and fully? No, he should not have done either of these things, for they would have given him no help. Just as he was, he went to Jesus, and with childlike sincerity and simplicity he poured out his heart before Him: "Lord, I believe. But, alas! There is still too much unbelief. Come to the help of my distrustfulness."

BREAKING FREE FROM INSINCERITY

Moreover, this teaches us what the only means of being delivered from insincerity is. The father felt that something in him was still waiting to believe, but he went to Jesus anyway and made it known to Him. He went to Jesus with the expectation that, in spite of his distrust, He would have mercy upon him and rescue him from it.

How utterly different this conduct is from that of so many people who are seeking faith. Year after year they continue mourning over insincerity, longing for sincerity, and yet they make no progress. Instead, they go on in their misery. They do not know

33

and they do not listen when they are told that genuine sincerity is simply to present ourselves just as we are, with all our unbelief. Repentance and healing will follow.

THE WAY TO RECEIVE HEALING

They ought to know that the only way to receive healing is to give themselves to the Savior, with the little bit of good that they have, even if that little bit is only a desire to believe. They can then give themselves to the Savior in spite of the excess of double-heartedness and worldly-mindedness and unbelief that yet remains in their hearts. Yes—to mourn unbelief, when actually dealing with Jesus—that is true sincerity.

Poor soul, if you have remained unrepentant and apart from the Lord out of fear of being insincere, you have grieved both the Lord and yourself by doing so. Even though you feel that you are ninety-nine percent unbelief and only one percent belief, go to Jesus with your feeble desire to believe. That is sincerity. Continue to pour out your heart every day before the Lord. Fight against your remaining insincerity and distrust at Jesus' feet. That is the only place where you can overcome. You may want to say aloud, "Lord, I believe. I will believe as well as I can. I believe at last that You are Jesus, the Helper of the wretched. Come to the help of my distrustfulness."

As you pray and strive every day in this manner, you will soon obtain the victory and the blessing. If you do not pray in this manner, however, you may be sure at least of this: as long as you remain apart

Faith and Repentance

from Jesus, no more sincerity will come. Remember, sincerity is the outpouring of the heart before the Lord, and it is obtained nowhere except in fellowship with Him and through His friendly grace.

HAVING THE FEAR OF GOD

One reason why we must be sincere and repentant before God is that He is an awesome Being. He deserves our sincerity, our entire heart repentance. Noah was acquainted with the awesomeness of God, as we see by Hebrews 11:7: *"By faith Noah,...moved with fear, prepared an ark."* There are many people who suppose that, when the Word of God says, *"Happy is the man that feareth alway"* (Prov. 28:14), it is commending a disposition in which unbelief becomes a sort of virtue. Of course, this "virtue" conflicts with the assurance and rest that are given by faith. Yet, they interpret this passage to mean that we must be afraid of this great and holy God. These people then fear their own weakness and unfaithfulness, and they dare not believe.

This view is altogether out of harmony with the Word of God. The Word teaches us that fear and confidence must go hand in hand. *"Many shall see it, and fear, and shall trust in the LORD"* (Ps. 40:3). *"Ye that fear the LORD, trust in the LORD"* (Ps. 115:11). *"Behold, the eye of the LORD is upon them that fear him, upon them that hope in his mercy"* (Ps. 33:18). Fear and confidence go together; the one increases the other.

This truth is set before us very clearly in the story of Noah. *"By faith Noah, being warned of God of things not seen as yet, moved with fear, prepared*

35

an ark" (Heb. 11:7). Noah's fear was partly the fruit of his faith and partly the force that made his faith active when he was building the ark. In other words, his fear was both a cause and an effect of his faith. He believed the announcement of the avenging flood; therefore, he feared. He feared the destruction that was to overtake his fellowmen, and he feared the holy God, from whom the judgment was to proceed. He feared; therefore, through faith he adhered to the promise of the ark and worked at it as the only means of preservation. Fear and trust were inseparable to him, the one indispensable to the other.

Anxious, unbelieving soul, you fear the Lord, you fear His holiness and His judgments, and you say that it is out of veneration for Him that you dare not believe or repent. You say that you are too unworthy in the presence of such a holy and dreadful God to claim the right of being called His child and of speaking to Him with confidence. Oh, how grievously you are mistaken!

UNBELIEF DISHONORS GOD

There is nothing that so much dishonors and angers the Lord as unbelief—not believing His Word, not believing that He has compassion on all the unworthy who come to Him in sincerity. There is nothing on which God sets His honor so much as on His free grace and His pity for the ungodly. You wound Him in the tenderest place when you doubt if His grace is indeed for you, and you drag its greatness and trustworthiness into doubt. O soul, when you fear the Lord, be even more afraid to dishonor Him by unbelief and unrepentance.

Faith and Repentance

But, no, you say that you do not doubt the Lord, but that you doubt yourself. You fear on account of your unfaithfulness, your insincerity. Do you not then understand that it is precisely this fear of yourself that is the strongest argument for your casting yourself upon the Lord and entrusting yourself to Him?

O soul, do not seek something in yourself any longer. If you wait until you no longer fear for yourself, you will never come to Christ at all. God never asks you for a promise to be faithful on which *He* can rely. No, instead He gives you a promise of faithfulness on which *you* can rely. Simply because you fear your own unfaithfulness, you must place your confidence in God's faithfulness.

THE GLORY OF GRACE

Herein lies the glory of free grace. The sinner, who cannot trust himself, who feels that he falls far short in everything—in faith, humility, earnestness, and sincerity—can still surrender himself to the Lord, as one who is utterly wretched, with confidence in the Word that he receives. God will keep such a soul. Yes, the sinner who fears his own failings must trust in the Lord. This is the only remedy. He has nothing on which he can hope except the promise of God's compassion. Every thought of fear must be a new reason for confidence.

Thus, he will learn that the fear of the Lord then becomes, through confidence, the source of peace and growing power, not of anxiety. This is shown in the Scriptures in Acts 9:31: *"The churches ...walking in the fear of the Lord, and in the comfort of the Holy Ghost, were multiplied."* He will also learn to fear no more, according to the words of the psalmist: *"Blessed is the man that feareth the LORD....His heart is established, he shall not be afraid"* (Ps. 112:1, 8).

Chapter 5

Becoming a
Child of God

*Yea, Lord: I believe that thou art
the Christ, the Son of God.
—John 11:27*

T he Lord had said to Martha, *"I am the resur-
rection, and the life: he that believeth in me,
though he were dead, yet shall he live"* (John
11:25). After that, He asked her, *"Believest thou
this?"* (v. 26). What answer was she to give? The
thought that her brother was to be raised again was
still too great and wonderful for her. And yet, she
knew that she believed in Jesus and did not doubt
Him or the things He said. What reply was she to
make?

With childlike simplicity and sincerity she said,
"'I believe that thou art the Christ,' though I do not
exactly know what I believe concerning the resurrec-
tion of my brother. I cannot fully understand, cannot
conceive of it. But, this I know: I have believed and
still believe in You, as the Son of the living God. You,
Your birth, Your power, and Your love, I do not
doubt."

39

How to Strengthen Your Faith

How instructive this picture of Martha's faith is! Imagine the Word of the Lord coming to a sinner with the promise of forgiveness and reception into a relationship with God. When he is asked, *"Believest thou this?"* (v. 26), the discouraged sinner falls, sighing, and answers, "Ah! no, I cannot yet believe this." After this, he proceeds to condemn himself—a thing that profits nothing—instead of acting as Martha did.

Martha did not yet believe everything, but what she did believe she spoke out before the Lord. She believed in Him as the Son of the living God; this was the principal thing and would prove to be the source of even greater faith. In connection with what she did believe, she was diligent in prayer. She was sincere both about what she believed and about what she was not sure of. By this means, her faith was strengthened and became capable of receiving still more and more.

Follow that example, you of little faith. Do you believe that your sins are forgiven, that you are a child of God, and that everlasting salvation is yours? Perhaps you are afraid to answer, "Yes." You see others who can say so. You read in God's Word that the Lord will give His grace so that you may be enabled to say so. But, you cannot say that salvation is yours, and you do not know how you will ever come to the point of daring to say so.

THE BEGINNINGS OF FAITH

In that case, learn the way from Martha. Do not continue to mourn over your unbelief. Instead, go to Jesus with that which you do believe. Although you cannot yet say, "He is my Savior," you at least know this: that your entire soul believes that He was sent by God to be a Savior and that He has proved Himself to be a Savior to others. Well, then, go with this confession to Jesus. Utter it before Him in prayer, look to Him, and adore Him as the Savior of the world. Speak out what you do believe, and by this means the faith in your heart will be confirmed and increased. Say, "Lord Jesus, how unbelieving I am! This, however, I do believe: that You are the Savior, full of love and grace, and mightily able to redeem."

Although you do not yet dare to say that Jesus is yours, forget yourself, and worship Him. In the midst of these exercises, your faith will increase, and, without being conscious of it, you will eventually come to know for sure that He is yours.

But, you must persevere, for as long as you cannot yet say, "He is mine, and I am His," let your soul make the ceaseless adoring confession, *"Yea, Lord: I believe that Thou art the Christ, the Son of God."* He will quickly confirm to you the following words of truth: *"Thou hast been faithful over a few things, I will make thee ruler over many things: enter thou into the joy of thy lord"* (Matt. 25:21). You will readily learn to believe, and then, like Martha, you will also see the glory of God.

FINDING FAITH

As I said, Martha was sincere about what she was not yet certain of. She most likely was eager to find out those things and to believe them. Christ has clearly taught us, *"Seek, and ye shall find"* (Luke 11:9). This is a sure and certain promise from our

Lord Jesus: everyone who truly seeks will certainly find and will become a child of God. Yet, there are so many people who apparently seek, sincerely and earnestly, and still complain that they do not find. What causes this failure?

Among other reasons, a principal cause is that they do not know what *finding* is. They have probably already found and yet continue to seek. This arises mainly from their not understanding that not only seeking and praying, but also finding, must take place by faith.

This matter may be clearer to you if I use an illustration. Suppose I have a large debt and must go to court because I cannot pay it. I search for a surety, one who will pay my debt for me. However, I cannot find one anywhere. Then I receive a letter from a friend who has heard of my misfortune, telling me that he will become my surety. He will come at the first opportunity to save me from being taken to court. Will I then deny that I have found someone who will pay my debt? Will I refuse to acknowledge that I have found him in no other way than by faith? I have not yet spoken to the man, I have not yet received the money, and yet out of trust in his letter and because I believe his word is sure, I may say, "I have found a surety."

Suppose, however, that the external realities in this case appear to be in conflict with faith. Suppose I am taken to court on account of my debt. My actual experience at that time, when I look around on the gloomy courtroom, might lead me to say, "I have no surety." Nevertheless, faith would still say, "I have found a surety. I know my friend will certainly come. I only have to wait a little while, and then he will put an end to the whole case." The real experience then comes later—after the finding.

CHRIST IS OUR SURETY

It is the same with the finding of the Lord Jesus. The awakened sinner searches all over for someone to pay his debt, to deliver his soul, but cannot find one. Then comes the Word of God with the message that Christ *"is the propitiation...for the sins of the whole world"* (1 John 2:2).

A man has only to receive that message, and then by faith he has found a Redeemer. The more he occupies himself with that message, and the more he is persuaded that the message is for him, the more he becomes strengthened in the conviction: "The Redeemer is also for me. God has said it." At last, he learns to say with gladness, "I have found the Savior." All this takes place simply and only by faith in the Word of God.

Yet, perhaps the sinner's experience is still in conflict with this confession. Suppose that he often feels very sinful, corrupt, and far away from God, as if he were in a gloomy dungeon. Consequently, he might ask, "If it is true that I have found the Savior, why do things happen this way for me?"

Even so, he remembers that the finding of the Redeemer precedes the real experience of redemption. He comforts himself with the thought that the Lord is honored by faith that holds fast to His Word as truth. It is by such a trial that faith begins to contemplate and to enjoy the presence of the almighty God. First comes the finding, then the receiving in faith, and then, later, the actual experience.

How to Strengthen Your Faith

Seeking soul, Jesus is waiting to be found. He is not far from you, but very near. You no longer need to seek Him. Rather, He seeks you. All you have to do is to believe this and say, "Jesus seeks me and is determined to find me." Let the word of God's grace fill your heart, and out of that word you will soon say in faith, "I have found Him whom my soul desires, Jesus, the Savior of sinners."

THE WORD IS IN YOUR MOUTH

You will certainly be able to say these words in faith, for once you have the Savior, *"the word is nigh thee, even in thy mouth, and in thy heart"* (Rom. 10:8). When writing to the Romans, Paul described the simplicity of faith and the salvation that is obtained by faith. Note his words in the following passage:

> *The righteousness which is of faith speaketh on this wise, Say not in thine heart, Who shall ascend into heaven? (that is, to bring Christ down from above): or, Who shall descend into the deep? (that is, to bring up Christ again from the dead). But what saith it? The word is nigh thee, even in thy mouth, and in thy heart: that is, the word of faith, which we preach.* (Rom. 10:6–8)

What is the meaning of this passage? Paul said to the Romans, "Do not seek faith in the heights above, the depths below, far off, or with great trouble, for *'the word is nigh thee, even in thy mouth, and in thy heart.'"* In other words, if you simply confess with your mouth that Jesus is Lord, and believe in your heart, you will be saved (v. 9).

44

Becoming a Child of God

How I wish that people would pay more attention to such words of God and understand that what God says is the truth. *"Hearken unto me, ye stouthearted, that are far from righteousness: I bring near my righteousness: it shall not be far off"* (Isa. 46:12–13). We are far from God, and yet the road to God is not long. We are just too weak and too blind to travel it.

Out of sheer compassion, God brings His salvation right up to us; He brings it very close to our hearts. He manifests His salvation, not in the heights and not in the depths, but in the innermost spirit of man. He sets it in our mouths and in our hearts, for Christ abides and comes to us in the preaching of the Word of faith.

And yet, so many go about seeking it, as if it were far off. How is it that they grieve at the thought of the majesty and the holiness of God, and why do they find it so impossible to climb up to Him to find a Savior for themselves? How is it that they speak of the Lord Jesus Christ as if He were still dead (although He did indeed die for our sins), as if He were not alive today to save them? I wish they did not think so.

In their lack of faith, they follow the righteousness of the law, which says that a man must do something before he can live with Christ. However, the message of the Gospel is, *"Receive with meekness the engrafted word, which is able to save your souls"* (James 1:21). Helpless and wretched, man has only to be silent and to receive. God brings the blessing near.

"The word is nigh thee, even in thy mouth, and in thy heart" (Rom. 10:8). Perhaps you mourn that it

45

is still not in your heart. Perhaps you are still afraid to simply speak it with your mouth. Nevertheless, observe how gracious God is. He will make the confession of your mouth the means of faith to your heart. Like Martha, you will speak out what you believe, you will admit what you do not yet believe, you will search for the way to believe those things, and then you will find it by the help of the Spirit.

TRANSFORMING YOUR HEART THROUGH WHAT YOU SAY

In the things of this world, we often teach our little children to utter words that they do not yet fully understand. We do this in sure confidence that the thoughts and feelings expressed in these words will gradually be imprinted on their hearts. Likewise, we constantly see idle and sinful words, which at the outset are uttered carelessly, become rooted in the heart of the speaker and bear their own fruits.

We may also observe something similar in prayer. The person who is constantly uttering the words, "Thy will be done," even though his heart does not yet fully assent to them, will be cleansed of an unwilling and antagonistic disposition simply by using the expression.

If only we dealt likewise with the salvation that is by faith! Take the Word into your mouth, humbly and earnestly. Repeat the words of grace, as if you heard the Lord God addressing them to you. Do not yield to the unbelief in your heart. Instead, combat and overcome it by attaching yourself to the Lord with the confession of your mouth. The consent of your heart will then surely be won.

Becoming a Child of God

You can do this now by continually thinking about and speaking what the Lord God has said to you: *"The word is nigh"* (Rom. 10:8). Confess it with your mouth, with longing and with prayer, so that it can eventually bring faith to your heart. Confess that Jesus is your choice and your Lord. The Spirit of God will work with the Word, and you will be able to believe with your heart. *"The word is nigh thee, even in thy mouth, and in thy heart"* (v. 8).

Chapter 6

Humility
and Penitence

Lord, I am not worthy that thou shouldest
come under my roof: but speak the word
only, and my servant shall be healed.
—Matthew 8:8

These words were spoken with a faith so great
that the Lord wondered at it and exclaimed,
"I have not found so great faith, no, not in Is-
rael" (Matt. 8:10). For those who desire to come to
faith, or who long for a stronger faith than they already have, it may be good to carefully examine the
faith of the centurion who spoke these words to
Christ.

Carefully observe the soil in which that great
faith had its roots. The soil was the soil of deep humility. This Gentile man was praised by the Jewish
elders as worthy of the Lord's favor. (See Luke 7:2–
5.) His faith surpassed all that the Lord had found in
Israel. Yet, this eminent man is the only one of
whom we read in the Gospels, during Jesus' sojourn
on earth, who did not consider himself worthy enough

for Jesus to enter his house. What wonderful humility in such a hero of faith! We learn the most momentous lesson from this: that deep humility and strong faith are knit to one another by the closest bonds.

Faith springs out of humility. When a man fully acknowledges that he has nothing and is content to receive favor as one who possesses nothing, then he casts himself on the free grace of God and receives that grace as one who believes. In the acknowledgment of his nothingness, this man does not dare to keep reminding God of his unworthiness, nor does he pester God with his desire for correction of certain failings in his life. Instead, because he has pleased such a great God to the point where He is prepared to show compassion to the poorest and most wretched sinner, he feels that nothing suits him better than to be silent and allow God to manifest His love.

Moreover, the sinner knows that he is so deeply corrupt that he can never become better through his own efforts. On this account, faith is the best proof of a man's humility. Out of the recognition of his utter helplessness, out of the knowledge that he can never become better, the sinner casts himself on the will of God.

HUMILITY IS FOUND IN BELIEF

This is entirely different from the theory that humility lies in not believing. There is no humility in waiting until something is found in us that could make us more acceptable to the Lord than we really are. And, there is no humility in refusing to obey

God's command to actually believe. Truly, humility is not found in these things. The idea that faith will eventually lead to pride is just as backward. No, as faith arises from humility, it will in turn only increase humility.

By his faith, the centurion recognized a power in Jesus that could heal the sick by His mere word. Jesus had such power over nature that the centurion felt himself to be unworthy to have Jesus in his house. And so it is with us. The more glorious faith's experience of the Lord's greatness and goodness becomes, the more deeply faith sinks into humility. The heart of a man then acknowledges the condescension by which such a God unveils Himself to such a sinner.

It always happens in this manner: the deeper the humility, the greater the faith. And, on the other hand, the stronger the faith, the deeper the humility. May the Lord teach us this truth: that there is no stronger proof of humility, and also no better means of increasing it, than faith. May He teach us, whether we feel deeply humbled or still desire to come to a deeper humility, that the one as well as the other should only draw us up to faith.

And now, soul, why do you not believe? Are you still too unworthy? Do not say so. The deeper your humility becomes, the stronger your reason and your right to believe will be. Are you still too proud? Do not be so any longer. Just bring yourself to the acknowledgment of your entire weakness, and confess that you are wholly lost. In the depths of your wretchedness, in all of your sinfulness, you will see that there is no other remedy than to let the Lord

help you and to commit yourself trustfully to the
Word of His grace.

RECOGNIZING YOUR OWN SINFULNESS

As I mentioned earlier in this chapter, some
people think that humility lies in continually reminding God of our unworthiness. However, this
does not bring us any closer to God. Of course, we
need to have a sense of the sin in our lives, but it
ought to bring us closer to Him. Note what happened to Peter.

By faith Peter had said, *"At thy word I will let
down the net"* (Luke 5:5), and Jesus wonderfully
blessed that faith. At the same time, the Savior
made Himself known as the mighty Ruler over nature, the beneficent Friend of His disciples. He unveiled His glory to Peter. And the fruit and the
result of all this grace was that Peter cast himself
before the Lord with the prayer: *"Depart from me;
for I am a sinful man"* (Luke 5:8).

The glory of the Lord appeared to him so
clearly in the light of his faith, and his own sinfulness became so manifest to him, that he uttered
this cry out of fear and self-abasement. This is clear
proof that the fruit of true faith is a sincere, inward
penitence and a deeper humiliation because of
one's sin.

This lesson is very important for many people
who wish to walk in faith. They think that they cannot fully believe because they are not yet deeply
enough convinced of sin. They do not seem to notice
that no one has defined how deeply a person must
feel sin before he may come to Jesus. There is no

standard of measurement for the depth of conviction. Rather, the first sense of need must bring us to Him.

INCREASING YOUR SENSE OF SIN

These people also do not understand that remaining apart from Jesus will only lessen their sense of sin. They do not understand how especially important it is that a developing faith become the means of increasing one's sense of sin. The following principle holds true: the closer to the light, the more visible the impurity. Likewise, the nearer we get to the Holy One, the stronger the sense of our unworthiness will be; the more blessed with grace, the deeper our conviction of sin.

As it was with Peter, so it is with all believers. The times in which Jesus' grace and love are most clearly revealed to us are the times in which we are most deeply humbled. And, for the most part, these times are not at the beginning, but in the later stages of the life of faith. Consider the case of Peter. He came to his deepest knowledge of sin when he denied his Lord. This occurred after he had already said, *"Thou art the Christ, the Son of the living God"* (Matt. 16:16).

Think of the covenant of grace that the Lord made with Jacob at Bethel. Yet, it was not until twenty years later that God first brought Jacob to the recognition of his sinfulness. It was in the crisis of the wrestling by night in which the Lord came to meet him as an antagonist, to break down the old nature and the power of the flesh.

Think also of David when he was a shepherd and fought against Goliath. In his youth, he tasted the glorious experiences of God's help and friendship. It was much later in life, long after he had become king, that he had to enter into the path of suffering before he could see sin unveiled. Likewise, there are still many people whom the Lord first leads to faith, and then, later on, He leads them through faith to the full knowledge of sin—to genuine penitence.

Consequently, if you desire to humble yourself and to turn back to God as one who is guilty, you must understand that doubt and unbelief will not help you, but will only hinder you in this. On the other hand, faith is the way to obtain all this fruit. If you doubt whether you indeed have faith, or if you can have it at all, you must consider that faith can flourish only in this poverty of the soul. While your feelings of unworthiness and guilt cause so much darkness and anxiety in the depths of your spirit, it is by this means that you will be driven to your Lord.

BECOMING LESS IN YOUR OWN EYES

The believer must never forget that two of the indispensable fruits and proofs of the sincerity of his faith are a constantly growing self-abhorrence and a lessening of himself in his own eyes. This is according to the Word of the Lord to His people:

> *"Thus saith the Lord...I will establish unto thee an everlasting covenant. Then thou shalt...be ashamed...when I am pacified toward thee for all that thou hast done.*   (Ezek. 16:59–61, 63)

Reader, why do you not believe? Surely you are not still waiting for more penitence and humility, for

penitence and humility are always the fruit of faith.
Believe today in the grace of Him who comes to you.
Everything that is lacking in you must stir you up to
this. With Him you receive everything that you are
seeking elsewhere in vain.

Chapter 7

The Certainty
of Faith

He staggered not at the promise of God through
unbelief...being fully persuaded that, what he
had promised, he was able also to perform.
—*Romans 4:20–21*

As you can see from this passage, Abraham did not doubt. This is a glorious testimony that should provoke us to jealousy and cause us to imitate his example. Here, the Word demonstrates to us the power by which Abraham obtained faith and silenced all doubts. The secret lay simply in the conviction that what God has promised, He is also able to perform.

On this account, Abraham was assured. Whenever doubts would arise, he always focused his eyes and mind on the incontrovertible argument that what has been promised, God is able to perform. This is why it was written:

Being not weak in faith, he considered not his
own body now dead...before him whom he be-
lieved, even God, who quickeneth the dead, and

How to Strengthen Your Faith

*calleth those things which be not as though they
were.   (Rom. 4:19, 17)*

Every time someone would ask, "How can these
things be?" this was his simple answer: "What God
has promised, He is able also to perform. There is
nothing too wonderful for the Lord. It is not my
business to be anxious or to ask how God's Word can
be fulfilled. The Lord will see to it."

My reader, you mourn over the power of your
doubts and say that you cannot overcome them.
Well, then, learn from Abraham's example how you
can do this. The first thing that is necessary is that
you understand and reflect upon the promise the
Lord has given you. If the Lord has given no promises to you, then it cannot be your duty to believe.
But, as surely as Scripture says, "Believe," there is
also a promise that has been given to you to believe.

Here is only one promise out of the thousands of
promises that are in the Scriptures: *"The Son of
man is come to seek and to save that which was lost"*
(Luke 19:10). God gives you the gracious promise
and commands you to believe it with all your heart.
It is His will that you receive it as the truth that His
Son has come for all who are lost, and therefore also
for you. He desires that you believe that His Son
seeks you and longs for you and that His Son will
save you.

God's will is that you ponder this thought and
cherish it in your heart until your whole soul stands
on this truth: "Jesus seeks me, as lost as I am; therefore, there is grace for me." As soon as you believe
that, the Savior will begin to come into you.

The Certainty of Faith

DO NOT CONSIDER YOUR FAILINGS

If you have now reached this first point, if you know that there is a promise also for you, then your second duty is not to look into yourself to find hope that what you expect to happen will take place. As Abraham did not regard his own body, which was already dead, so you must not regard your own dead soul. Although you feel yourself to be dead, powerless, insincere, and very sinful; although you are lacking in penitence, earnestness, and everything else that you know you ought to have, still act like Abraham. Believe in God, who makes the dead alive and calls things that are not as though they were (Rom. 4:17). Act like Abraham and cast down every doubt with the thought: "What God has promised, He is able also to perform." Keep your mind occupied with this certain truth: He is come to save that which was lost, and there is no one so far lost that Jesus cannot find him and save him.

It comes simply to two points. First, know that there is a promise for you, lost sinner. Then, secondly, adhere simply to this fact: what has been promised, He is able also to perform. Say to Him, "*Lord, I believe; help thou mine unbelief*" (Mark 9:24). I will no longer dishonor You by doubting. I will adore and trust Your power, love, and faithfulness. I will venture to surrender my soul to You. Although I do not feel it, I will believe it. You seek and save that which is lost. Lord, help me, for I do believe."

THE STABILITY OF FAITH

Many people think that faith is something that, at its best, is still very uncertain. They believe it to be less certain, for example, than sight or hearing. They seem to think that faith is a sort of imagination by which we try to be assured in our hearts that we will be saved. The result of this misconception is that they often attempt to exercise faith, but find no rest in it, or perhaps even come to regard all assurance of faith as conjecture, self-deception, or presumption. They do not understand what faith is, that it is *"the substance* [assurance] *of things hoped for"* (Heb. 11:1).

The epistle to the Hebrews should have made the definition of faith very clear to such people. In that epistle, faith is represented as the highest certainty, as a sure foundation on which one can build and safely trust one's self. In faith, there is nothing that changes or can be changed. Abraham saw that faith is a strong basis, for the simple reason that faith depends upon what exists more firmly than rocks or mountains, namely, the Word of God.

Heaven and earth will pass away, but the Word of God endures to eternity (Matt. 24:35). On this account, in order to come to rest, peace, and stability, the sinner simply has to ask, "What has God said? Is there anything that God has commanded me to believe? Has He spoken anything that is directed to every sinner and that every sinner is bound to believe? If so, then it is my duty to search this out and receive it as being the Word of the true God, and therefore sure and certain."

What is it, then, that every sinner is to believe? Simply this: that Christ has been given to us by God as our Savior. *"This is a faithful saying, and worthy of all acceptation, that Christ Jesus came into the world to save sinners"* (1 Tim. 1:15). This refers to all sinners without distinction, even the chief of sinners. Let the sinner who longs to be saved only hold fast to that truth and be occupied with it. Let him go out of himself and be surrounded with this thought until his heart is filled with it: "Jesus came to save sinners, even me."

Christ is certainly for everyone. He did not come because we have believed all this or have been converted. No, He came because we are ungodly. And, whether you believe it or not, it remains true that Christ is offered by God also to you.

Even before you believe it, it is the truth. The truth of it does not depend on anything in you that is yet to take place. Rather, it is rooted in the fact that God has said it. Remember, what God has promised, he is able also to perform. Therefore, there is nothing for you to do but to hear according to the Word of God and to receive it in your soul until it becomes a settled conviction. It must be true; Christ is a Savior also for you, for God has said it.

FAITH, THE FIRM FOUNDATION

If anyone questions you, "Are you already converted?" or "Are you worthy of it?" or "Are you indeed sincere?" you may silence him with the simple answer: "Whoever or whatever I may be, Christ is for the sinner, and so He is also for me." The more you accustom yourself day by day to ask simply, "Am I sure that God has said it?" the more you will experience faith as a firm foundation. Standing on this basis, you cannot waver, but you will come to an ever-clearer insight into the truth that faith is nothing but a receiving and committing of oneself to the Word of the true God. Hence, faith is a firm foundation, and it cannot be otherwise.

And now, anxious one, why do you not believe? Faith does not come by simply imagining that you, too, are a chosen one. Rather, faith involves laying yourself down on the immovable rock of the Word of the Lord. *"God so loved the world"* (John 3:16) that *"Christ died for the ungodly"* (Rom. 5:6). And now, He comes to ask you, *"If I say the truth* [to you], *why do ye not believe?"* (John 8:46). See to it, I entreat you, that you give Him an answer.

Chapter 8

The Surrender
of Faith

First [they] *gave their own*
selves to the Lord.
—2 Corinthians 8:5

I n fulfillment of His promise, the Lord gives Himself to us through the gracious working of His Spirit. Through faith, we receive Him and know that He is ours. This faith, while going out from our hearts to meet Jesus, is at the same time a surrender to Him. We can never receive the Savior and His grace without simultaneously surrendering ourselves to Him to be sealed and filled with salvation. Through faith, we know that the Lord is ours because His Word tells us that He gives Himself to us. Likewise, we also know through faith that God receives us as His own. His Word assures us of that.

TWO SIDES OF FAITH

Faith, therefore, has two sides: the believing reception of the Lord Jesus with all that He gives, and the believing surrender of all that one has to the Lord. The one side cannot occur without the other. If I take Jesus as my Savior to free me from sin, I must also take Him as King to rule over me. He cannot perform His work in me if I do not surrender myself to Him. Thus, assurance in Jesus is, at the same time, a committal of oneself to Him.

Notice once again the simplicity of faith. If you wish to know what you have to do, the answer is, "Give yourself to the Lord Jesus." Give yourself to the Lord Jesus just as you are. You have to give yourself to Him, not as an offering that is worthy of Him, not as one who is already His friend and on whom He can look down with complacency. No, you have to surrender yourself to Him as one who is dead, as a sinner whom He must save and make alive again.

The magnitude of your sins, the corruption that you feel struggling within you, the very insincerity of your coming to Him, are not reasons why you should not venture to give yourself to Him. No, just the opposite. These are proof that you stand in need of a Savior. Indeed, the Word of God tells us that Jesus came on behalf of those who experience such things. O sinner, just as you are, surrender yourself to Jesus.

COMPLETE SURRENDER

Surrender yourself to Him wholly and undividedly. Hold nothing back that is yours. Do not think that He is to do one part of the work and you are to do the rest. No, submit entirely to His estimate of you. Although you do not yet feel the power to separate yourself from all sins, although you still feel that your heart is attached to one thing or another, confess all this before Him. It is also through the confession of sins that we surrender ourselves to Him.

Understand that the more you surrender yourself entirely to Him, the more completely He is able to accomplish His work in you. Think of His complete surrender for you and to you. Think of the claim of His love upon you and the complete salvation with which He will fill you, and let your surrender to Him be complete and undivided.

And, above all, surrender yourself to Him in faith. Perhaps you have given yourself to Him before this, but it brought you no peace, for you did not know if the surrender was accepted by Him. You wanted a sign from heaven, a divine confirmation in your heart to tell you that He had accepted you. But this was wrong. He has said, *"Him that cometh to me I will in no wise cast out"* (John 6:37). God has said, *"Return, ye backsliding children, and I will heal [you]"* (Jer. 3:22). When you surrender yourself to Jesus, you must believe that He will not cast you away; you must find assurance in God's Word. You are to take your stand upon it, because God speaks the truth.

However wretched you are, however imperfect your surrender is, it must be a surrender of faith, of faith that He receives you, because He has said it. Although you find it difficult to believe that so firmly, although it seems very hazardous to you who is so great a sinner, it is, nevertheless, your duty to believe that He receives you when you surrender yourself to Him.

Do not set yourself above God. Do not say, "I have done my part, but I do not know if God will do His." No, think of the Word. Say to the Lord that it is on His promise that you surrender yourself. Fill your life every day with the faithfulness of God's promise, and you will gradually come to the blessed certainty that He receives you. Yes, you will even be able to say, "He has received me."

SURRENDER THROUGH OBEDIENCE

Perhaps you say that you would gladly surrender yourself to Him, that it is your earnest and sincere desire to belong to the people of the Lord, but you are kept back, and you yourself do not really know the reason why. Perhaps it is not quite clear to you what you have to do when you surrender your life completely to Christ. You do not yet understand the simplicity of faith, and you do not see that it is something that you can and must do without the least delay. Let us try to understand this by the example of Abraham, the father of the faithful.

The Lord had said to Abraham, *"Get thee out of thy country...unto a land that I will show thee"* (Gen. 12:1). In this calling of Abraham, we find a divine command and a divine promise. The command is, *"Get thee out of thy country"*; the promise is, *"'I will show thee'* another land." Hebrews 11:8 tells us, *"By faith Abraham, when he was called...obeyed; and he went out."*

If he had not believed the promises, if he had not believed that the Lord would certainly bring him to that unknown land, Abraham would surely never have gone out. His faith in the promise was his power to obey the command. He did not first go out of his land and then become a believer afterward. For, if he had not first believed that he would find that foreign country, he would never have had the courage to leave his fatherland. He first believed, and then he went out.

God calls you also, my reader, to get out of the life of sin and to leave the world behind. He calls you to surrender all your wants and desires to Him. However, it is as if the call did not succeed with you. You are afraid that you will never reach heaven. It is as if you lack the courage and the strength to tread that way. It is no wonder. Abraham, too, would never have had the courage to abandon everything and to undertake that long journey, if he had not held fast to the Word of God: *"a land that I will show thee"* (Gen. 12:1). Every consideration of the sacrifice, the folly, and the dangers of going to an unknown land was overcome by the thought, "I go to a country that God will show me." Faith was Abraham's strength. Faith must also be your strength. Like Abraham, you, too, must learn to adhere to God's command that is given, so that you may say, *"The LORD...brought me thither"* (Ezek. 40:1).

THE PROMISES ARE YOURS

"But, I have not received the promises," you cry. My reply is, "You have indeed received the promises." God is not unfair; He would never say that you must go to heaven without the promise that He will bring you there. He does not ask you to surrender everything without also promising you that He will supply all your needs (Phil. 4:19). He has given you

Jesus to show you the new country and to lead you on the path to righteousness. He does not say, "Repent," without pointing to Jesus, whom He ordained to give repentance. He does not say, "Abandon sin, and be saved," without at the same time saying, "Jesus frees and saves from sin." It is only in the strength of this faith that you will enter heaven.

Therefore, observe the calling of God for your life. Understand that Jesus will do all for you. Receive Him today as your Guide, given by God, who will direct you on the way. However wretched you are, just simply believe that it is true that God has given His Son, Jesus, also to you to save you. Be willing, and acknowledge Him as your Savior. Rejoice in the thought that God has given Him to the sinner and thus also to you.

Although you still feel nothing in yourself, firmly grasp this thought the whole day. Carry it around with you in the midst of all your work. Say, "It is certainly true that God has given Jesus also to me to save me." This simple thought is faith. Hold fast to it, and thank God for it. It will quickly send forth roots in you, and you will rejoice in the assurance that Jesus is leading you to heaven. Having been called, you, too, will be obedient because of your faith.

AN EXAMPLE OF OBEDIENCE TO FAITH

The story of Naaman's healing has always served as a striking illustration of the way of faith. Naaman himself is to us a clear example of all the humbling and offensive features that faith has for the natural heart. Second Kings 5:10 says, *"And El-isha sent a messenger unto him, saying, Go and wash in Jordan seven times."*

When Naaman received the message of the prophet, his response was entirely in accordance with the expectations of human nature. Human nature always expects to see something, to receive something in the form of external ceremonies. Naaman's answer was,

> *Behold, I thought, He will surely come out to me, and stand, and call on the name of the LORD his God, and strike his hand over the place, and recover the leper.* (2 Kings 5:11)

In this verse, we see the expectations of someone who sought healing. Naaman wanted a visible, impressive revelation of the Lord's power, something revealed to his senses. Yet, when a servant was sent with the simple message of faith, he turned away disappointed, as if this were no answer to his prayer.

Notice the contents of the message: Naaman was told to wash in the Jordan. Water appeared to be the means of healing. Yet, was the Damascus not larger than the Jordan, and was it not better than all the waters of Israel? Naaman did not know that it was not the water that would heal him, but the power of God through His Word. Nor did he understand that his surrender to God's method was necessary for his healing.

CLEANSED BY FAITH ALONE

In like manner, one who seeks salvation cannot understand that he is cleansed by faith alone. The waters of a deep and inward penitence, the streams of sincere humility, and the loyalty of an inner love—are these not enough to cleanse one from his sins? Why is faith named above these? Many people try to set themselves above mere faith, as if God had not called that which is weak and despised and indeed nothing; as if He had not chosen faith as the way in which man, as capable of no achievement, was to receive everything out of free compassion.

Submission to mere faith is a difficult task for many people. They must be taught to surrender to the obedience of faith. In Naaman's case, more than anything else, the washing seven times was sure to prove a stumbling block. If the waters were good, why was one washing not sufficient? If the healing did not take place at the fifth or sixth time, why should it occur just at the seventh time? Reason was thoroughly entitled to inquire in this fashion.

Nevertheless, faith cannot insist on an answer to these questions and at the same time obey what God says through His prophets. This submission should become a very significant instance in the longsuffering of faith. It should remind us of how faith is to hold out, although it does not see the least sign of change or healing. It should teach us the lesson that is learned with so much difficulty: that there must be a continual repetition of the act of faith, holding fast to the Word of God, until He bestows the blessing.

SUBMISSION TO FAITH BRINGS SALVATION

You who are seeking salvation, learn from this example. When you submit to what does not appear to you to be the best means, to what seems too small and trifling for such a great result, you will have faith. Through the continuous repetition of what at the outset seems fruitless, you will be called on to persevere in faith.

I hope I have made it clear to you that faith is God's way. It was God who devised it, not man. On this account, faith is a stumbling block to every Naaman, until he learns to bow beneath the Word of God as one who is helpless.

Surrender yourself to God, therefore, and receive what He says: *"He that believeth...shall be saved"* (Mark 16:16). Go every day to the Word and its streams of living water. Although it seems to you somewhat trifling to wash there, to plunge and bathe in its streams, to receive from it this or that promise, and to do the very same thing every day anew without experiencing any healing, hold on.

Persevere, and the blessed result will be like that of Naaman. *"His flesh came again like unto the flesh of a little child, and he was clean"* (2 Kings 5:14). It was as if he was born a second time. You also will be born again by the living Word and will be cleansed from your sin. This cleansing does not lie in you, or even in the Word itself, but in the faithfulness of God, who has said, *"Whosoever believeth on him shall not be ashamed"* (Rom. 9:33). Therefore, surrender to Him and obey Him through faith, and be cleansed and healed.

Chapter 9

Receiving and Nourishing Faith

O woman, great is thy faith:
be it unto thee even as thou wilt.
—Matthew 15:28

It is well-known that nothing on earth is so desirable as great faith. Many people may wish to have it and may pray for it, and yet there are few who come to possess it. Why?

HOW CHRIST WILL BRING YOU TO FAITH

A principal reason is that they refuse to walk in the way that leads to faith. They are afraid of the school where that faith is taught. Or, they have very wrong ideas concerning the way to attain that great faith.

For instance, they sometimes think of faith as if it were a gift that is bestowed all at once. Their thoughts are so backward that, when the Lord hears their prayers and is about to lead them in another direction than they had expected, they suppose that

He is no longer caring for them. And so, you who desire more faith, learn from the Canaanite woman. Matthew 15:28, quoted above, illustrates how the Lord will bring you to great faith.

He Will Test You

First of all, He will test and try you. The Canaanite woman had a daughter possessed by a devil, and what a trial that was to her! The Lord still sends His children trials, though they may be of very different kinds. One man may have a trial in the physical life. Another may have difficulty in his family. Still another may experience inward vexation of his soul. And with another, the trial may be a hidden conflict with sin. Nevertheless, there must be a trial. For, as long as the flesh has everything agreeable and according to its inclinations, the soul will never wholly and with power cling to the Lord.

By necessity, the sinner is driven to seek all his salvation in the Lord and to commit himself to Him. Blessed trial! It is the message of God to teach more faith. Yet so many people regard the trial as the messenger of His wrath and aversion, instead of humbly allowing themselves to be led by its hand to the Lord.

He Will Leave Your Prayers Unanswered

When the Lord is going to lead someone to great faith, He not only tests him, but He also leaves his prayers unanswered. This is what happened with the Canaanite woman. For a time He did not answer her, and when He finally did reply to her, the answer was still more unfavorable than His silence had been.

This is always the way God deals with us. If the answer to every prayer came immediately, how would we ever become acquainted with the Lord Himself? The gifts of God would occupy our attention so much that we would overlook the Lord Himself. Each of us must first be put to the test, as to whether or not we can stand upon the Lord and what He has provided without any answer. It is a test of whether God and His Word are sufficient for us.

Indeed, God tests us, not so that we will doubt His love, but rather so that we will commit to it, even when His Word appears to be opposed to it. A faith so great that it still clings to the Lord, in spite of apparent rejection, is acceptable to Him above all else. This precious lesson is learned and practiced only in the conflict of unanswered but persevering prayer.

He Will Humble You

Once more, the man who is to come to great faith must be humbled. What harsh words were spoken to the poor heathen woman: *"It is not meet to take the children's bread, and cast it to dogs"* (Matt. 15:26)! However, she accepted Christ's words and used them as her strongest argument. She overcame the Lord with His own weapons and turned His rejection into her plea: *"Yet the dogs eat of the crumbs which fall from their masters' table"* (v. 27).

You, likewise, must do the same. When your sins are laid bare to you, when your unworthiness is held up before you, and when the Word makes you feel that you are an ungodly and accursed sinner, always answer with the woman: "Yes, Lord, I am very wretched. All that my heart testifies of sin is true. *'Yet,* [even] *the dogs eat.'* And, with such a Lord as You, there is overflowing grace even for the most wretched sinner."

Trees become stronger as their roots grow deeper. Faith and humility also work by this principle: the deeper the descent of humility, the stronger the faith. When the Lord has humbled you, your faith will lean wholly on the Lord, not half on itself.

Observe, then, that this is Jesus' school for faith. Do not be grieved if the lessons are sometimes heavy; He has told you of this beforehand. Nevertheless, hold fast to this conviction: when your soul is brought into trial, when your sin and unworthiness become more distinct and press you deeper down, look upon all this as the way along which the all-loving Jesus will lead you to the life of faith, in which He takes such delight. And, when you are dispirited, read again the story of the Canaanite woman, and be strengthened by the glorious victory and reward of her conflict of faith. The more difficult the school, the more glorious the prize.

KEEPING FAITH NOURISHED

Once Christ brings you to faith, you must diligently nurture it. The lessons that are learned through tests and trials help to keep faith nourished throughout the Christian walk, but faith does not survive unless you nourish it continually with the Word of God. I will illustrate this principle with the story of the Israelites, when God gave them manna in the wilderness.

In the silence and coolness and secrecy of the night, God gave the manna. *"And they gathered it every morning, every man according to his eating: and when the sun waxed hot, it melted"* (Exod. 16:21). In the freshness and lively activity of the morning hour, the people had to go out to gather it. It was thus the first task of each day to receive bread from God's hand. For, when the sun waxed hot and warmed the earth, the manna melted and was no longer to be found. They did not receive this hidden manna in the glow of the midday sun, or in the hustle and bustle of the day, but in the charming coolness of the morning, before the mind was ensnared by the seductions of the world.

This is a lovely and instructive image of the way in which God still gives nourishment for our faith. I am convinced that there are many people who sincerely desire a confirmation of faith, yet they have not become partakers of it because they do not search for it at all times. How many people only read the Bible in the evening? After the freshness of the morning hour and the strength of the day have been devoted to the world, they come to God in the evening, weary in mind and body, to serve Him with the remnant of their energies. No wonder there is no blessing enjoyed! The heart is weary; the tenderness of the spirit and its receptiveness for the Word are dulled.

On the other hand, there are many Christians who are content with a general reading of the Word in the morning, without privately searching the Scripture, without reflecting or meditating on it with

How to Strengthen Your Faith

prayer. This still yields little blessing. Reading a chapter once a day is, as a rule, not sufficient. No, anyone who truly desires to increase in faith must see to it that he endeavors in the morning hour to gather manna, or spiritual food, on which he can ponder for the rest of the day.

He who goes out in the morning without partaking of this spiritual food will come home weary in the evening, with little desire to eat. And, he who does not first lay up the Word in his heart in the morning should not be surprised if the world assumes the first and chief place in his heart, for he has neglected the only means of being ahead of the world.

The Lord gives us the night so that we may throw off the weariness of the day, and in the morning hour we may make a new beginning with fresh spirit and energy. Likewise, the believer must take and devote to the Lord his first fresh and undiminished forces. He must gather his manna while the blessing of the night's rest is upon him and before the corruption of the world has again banished its lovely dew.

Remember, once the sun has warmed the earth, the manna will melt. Likewise, the life of grace will not endure the heat of the world unless it is first strengthened by food. When the heat of the day has come and temptation has first passed over the soul, all the gladness and trustfulness of the morning hour have also passed away.

"Cause me to hear thy lovingkindness in the morning" (Ps. 143:8). *"My voice shalt thou hear in the morning, O LORD; in the morning will I direct my prayer unto thee, and will look up"* (Ps. 5:3).

Receiving and Nourishing Faith

Such words as these show us the attitude of the believer who is, first and chiefly and with his whole heart, earnestly trying to serve the Lord. With every morning hour, he will taste the delightful experience of the Word. *"His going forth is prepared as the morning"* (Hos. 6:3).

Reader, why do you not believe? Be faithful toward yourself and toward God. There is no piety in mourning over your unbelief unless you also lay aside everything that stands in the way of faith. If the irregular, superficial use of the Word, or the giving of the first, the fresh, the best hours of the day and energies of the soul to the world and its service is the cause, then come. Make a change in these areas of your life. Morning by morning go and seek your God. He will not keep Himself hidden from you, no matter what trials and tests you may eventually face.

MAINTAINING THE SPIRITUAL LIFE

The Lord said to the Israelites,

I will rain bread from heaven for you; and the people shall go out and gather a certain rate every day, that I may prove them, whether they will walk in my law, or no. (Exod. 16:4)

This verse is not only an instruction to the Israelites, but it is also a Scripture that is applicable to Christians today. In these words, we have the rule for the maintenance of the spiritual life, as well as the law for the growth and increase of the life of faith.

This law is in no respect different from what we observe in the natural life every day. We all know how little children are fed so that they will grow up to be strong men and women. Yet, even the strong man has to maintain his strength through nourishment. A little food each day gives strength of body.

It is thus with everything in nature. The little tree becomes large; the poor man becomes rich; the grandest building rises from its foundation; the longest journey can be performed, not with great and violent strides, but by the silent, persevering faithfulness of little, invisible progress each day.

"A certain rate every day." This general rule of the natural life also prevails in the spiritual. And yet, there are so many Christians who, by not acknowledging this, suffer dreadful loss. They imagine that great exertion of strength at particular times, or fervent prayers when they feel stirred up, are the means of securing the increase and the flourishing of the spiritual life. However, they do not understand the golden rule: *"a certain rate every day,"* the day-by-day, regular consumption of spiritual food by which the soul obtains its growth.

They have not yet comprehended the lesson that faith and the life of faith must have nourishment or daily bread. They still do not realize that with the promise, *"I will rain bread from heaven,"* there also stands the command: *"The people shall go out and gather a certain rate every day, that I may prove them, whether they will walk in my law, or no."*

Beloved reader, have you not often mourned the unstable and changeable character of your spiritual life? Have you not often wondered why days of hope are so short-lived? And, have you not often asked what you should do first so that things would change, so that your faith might abide and increase?

LIFE IS DRAWN FROM THE WORD

It would not surprise you that you would be weak if your body was deprived of food for a couple of days. Does it then surprise you that your faith would not be living, firm, and strong if you do not faithfully partake of the Word of God each day? That is the nourishment for faith: from it, and from it alone, does faith draw its strength.

"Man shall not live by bread alone, but by every word that proceedeth out of the mouth of God" (Matt. 4:4). Confess that you yield too often to one worldly circumstance or another, that you fall into idleness and apathy, and that you neglect the silent meditation upon God's Word. Admit that you use His Word so hastily and superficially that your soul is not nourished. No wonder you have to mourn a leanness in your soul! Begin today, and from now on let no day pass by without eating the heavenly manna: the Word of God and the living Christ in the Word.

God gave manna every day in the wilderness, up until the homecoming in Canaan. In the same manner, if we go out and gather the manna of the Word, we will find instruction, strengthening, purification, and salvation for every new day.

Receive the Word in faith. The one who continues day by day with faithful perseverance in the Word will experience the increase of faith. Although it is unobserved and slow, although one does not at once observe the blessing that flows from it, the increase is certain and sure.

How to Strengthen Your Faith

GUARDING YOUR FAITH

Yes, your faith will surely and certainly increase, but you must be especially careful that the Devil does not come and take it away from you. *"Then cometh the devil, and taketh away the word out of their hearts, lest they should believe and be saved* (Luke 8:12).

The Lord teaches us that when the Devil is determined to hold anyone back from salvation, he merely has to keep him back from faith. Then, the person will not be prepared for salvation. In order to keep anyone back from faith, the Devil simply has to take away the Word from the heart. Then the person will not believe. Therefore, you must guard your faith.

As far as the Word is concerned, so many people fall into the hands of the Devil, even though they say they desire to believe. This is a dreadful thought. To the Devil, it is of little importance in what particular way this takes place, as long as he can take the Word out of the heart. He does this in many ways.

Stay Clear of Sin and Unrighteousness

In one case, the Enemy can accomplish the theft of the Word by all manner of sin and unrighteousness. The love of sin cannot dwell together with the Word. The heart cannot simultaneously move toward God and away from God. It cannot equally desire the Word and sin. One or the other of these must be cast out. Alas! How many times does a sinner who said that he was seeking Jesus, and who desired to believe, let slip God's Word that he had laid up in his heart in the morning! This happens because he is not willing to say farewell to his sin, anger, lying, deception, envy, or impurity.

Be Free of Worldly Cares

In another case, the Word is stifled by worldly cares and inclinations. It may be the heavy sorrow and anxiety of one who has a difficult lot in the world, or it may be the temptation and preoccupation with the world that often springs from prosperity. Nevertheless, how constantly it happens that the Word is stifled, and thus taken away, by love of the world!

Focus on God, Not Yourself

Again, there are others from whom the Devil easily takes the Word away because they are so occupied with themselves and their sins. Instead of the heart being kept focused on the Word of promise, the heart is fixed on its own innermost workings. These people are so involved with their own feelings, their own wretchedness and weakness, their efforts to be converted in their own strength, that the Word is loosely held and easily carried away.

Think of how superficially the Word is read. Think of what little effort is often made to understand the Word, to take it into the heart and keep it there every day in order to strengthen one's faith. It is no wonder that the Word is lightly and easily taken away! It costs the Devil little effort.

Reader, if you are seeking Jesus, if you want to come to faith, be admonished by this earnest Scripture: *"Then cometh the devil, and taketh away the word...lest they should believe"* (Luke 8:12). Whatever temptation there may be, either from the world or in your own heart, remember to always keep and cling to the Word. Do not let the Devil take it away from you. Let the precepts and promises of the Word be your meditation day and night. *"Let the word of Christ dwell in you richly"* (Col. 3:16).

The language of David must be yours: *"Thy word have I hid in mine heart...it is my meditation all the day"* (Ps. 119:11, 97). Then, when you have found life, you will later on also be able to say as he did, *"This I had, because I kept thy precepts"* (v. 56).

Seeking soul, even the Devil knows that where the Word dwells in the heart, faith arises. Learn this, and be assured that faith will awaken in you as you humbly and silently hold fast to the living Word of God. God Himself has said that it is the Word *"which is able to save your souls"* (James 1:21). As the Word is received and kept in this hope, He is faithful to bestow the blessing of the Word by the Spirit.

The Evil One retreats before that Word, just as he did before the *"It is written"* (Matt. 4:4) that came out of Jesus' mouth. With and by that Word, the Lord God and His Spirit come to the heart of one who seeks.

Chapter 10

Justification:
By Faith or by Works?

Therefore we conclude that a man is
justified by faith without the
deeds of the law.
—Romans 3:28

T he Lord has revealed to us two ways that lead us to Him and salvation. In one, the law leads us; in the other, grace does. Both ways are good and come from God. However, there is only one of the two for us to use, because of our weaknesses. The law is good for those who have the power to obey and to follow it. Grace, on the other hand, is the way for those who are powerless and can accomplish nothing.

GRACE VERSUS THE LAW

There are many differences between the law and grace. The law makes demands that must be fulfilled; grace gives and needs simply to be received. The law says, "Do this, and you will live." Grace says, "Believe, and you will be saved." The law demands works, yet it gives no strength to perform them; grace asks for faith, which it awakens by its own power. This faith is nothing but the acknowledgment of weakness and a consent to be willing to receive everything for nothing. The law directs us to a mountain too steep to climb; grace directs us to the valley, where we only have to sink down to be preserved.

It is of the utmost importance that we know the difference between these two ways, choose the right one, and walk in it. For, in our present, sinful condition, there is only one of these ways that is still really of service to us, although men would just as gladly walk in the other. It is good for us that God has left us in no doubt as to which one is wished for and approved of by Him.

JUSTIFIED BY FAITH?

It was especially the apostle Paul whom God chose to clearly point out to us the way of salvation—as he did most fully in his epistle to the Romans. The conclusion of his teaching is the text quoted at the beginning of this chapter: *"Therefore we conclude that a man is justified by faith without the deeds of the law."* Paul showed how all mankind, Jews as well as Gentiles, had missed the glory of God. They could not fulfill—they did not wish to fulfill—the law of God.

The law must be perfectly obeyed; otherwise, it works only wrath. The law knows nothing about grace; it knows only what is right. God has searched the world, and there is not even one person who is righteous (Rom. 3:10). By the law, every mouth was stopped, and the whole world was made guilty before God (v. 19). The law itself declared that, *"By the deeds of the law there shall no flesh be justified"* (v. 20). *"But the just shall live by his faith"* (Hab. 2:4). By the death of Christ, God reconciled the world. He allowed the punishment and the demands of the law to be fulfilled through His Son.

God has permitted an everlasting and infinite righteousness to be brought into the situation. God offers it to us for nothing. *"Without money and without price"* (Isa. 55:1), this righteousness is ours through the free gift of God. In the case of the corrupt, curse-deserving, and powerless sinner, there can be no talk of service or works, but only talk of faith.

As I said earlier, faith is submission and surrender, particularly to the righteousness of God. Where that faith in Jesus and the Word of His grace is found, there the sinner is made partaker of the righteousness of God. Faith is simply the eye that sees God's righteousness as it was offered, the hand that receives it, and the activity that takes hold of it for oneself. He who believes is justified, for *"a man is justified by faith."*

What folly, then, it is to still look to one's own works of merit. Sinner, are you resolved to work for your salvation? Then you must keep the whole law, and keep it perfectly. But, even if you do, you will certainly be condemned. Do you desire to be justified? Only believe in Christ and His righteousness, in God and the promises of His grace. His promises are intended for you. By that faith, you will be justified *"without the deeds of the law."*

How to Strengthen Your Faith

JUSTIFIED BY WORKS?

But let us now look at the other side of justification. James wrote, *"Ye see then how that by works a man is justified, and not by faith only"* (James 2:24). It has often been supposed that there is a contradiction between this utterance of James and the doctrine of Paul, which we dealt with in the first half of this chapter. Yet, when we realize that the works of which Paul wrote are entirely different from those that James intended, we see that there is no contradiction at all. Paul always spoke of the works of the law, whereas James had his eyes upon the works of faith.

The works of the law are those that are done out of the individual power of man. They are intended to fulfill the law of God in order to earn His favor. By the works of the law, a man tries to make himself worthy of that favor. However, the Word of God says that man is justified without the works of the law. He can do nothing that is good or meritorious; all that comes from him is impure and deserving of wrath.

On the contrary, the works of faith, of which James wrote, are those that must be done for the confirmation and the perfection of faith. They are done out of the power that God gives and are not intended to merit anything. They serve to manifest all that faith has received from free grace. They follow conversion, while the works of the law can only precede conversion.

The works of the law glorify man, but the works of faith give God all the honor, for they are done in the acknowledgment of personal unworthiness. Works and faith go together, for they are both fruits of grace and signs of the renewing of the mind—faith is the root of the works, and the works perfect the faith.

THE SOLUTION: WORKS OF FAITH

In this way, it can now be clearly understood why the Word of God says, *"To him that worketh not, but believeth on him that justifieth the ungodly, his faith is counted for righteousness"* (Rom. 4:5), but also insists on works. The works that are done apart from faith, as an endeavor to make ourselves worthy of God's favor, are not to be done. Such works keep us back from faith, which is the reception of God's free grace. Works without faith are abominable in the eyes of God. According to the Scripture, one who does not do the works of the law can still be justified.

The works that are done with and in faith, however, are acceptable to God. Such works of faith must be done, and the more the better. It is by these Spirit-inspired works that *"a man is justified"* (James 2:24). They are the manifestation of a faith that actually bears fruit, and not merely of a faith that continues to be inactive and is thus dead.

Let anyone who seeks to come to Jesus in faith thus understand what is to be thought of works. As soon as he begins to look upon his works as the basis of merit, as soon as he begins to say in fear, "My works are too small, too trifling, too sinful for me to be received," he must remember at once that *"God imputeth righteousness without works"* (Rom. 4:6). With a sense of his unworthiness, a man commits himself to the gracious promises of God because he hopes or knows that the Lord receives him apart from his merits. He seeks, instead, to praise God for whatever merits he may have.

No sin or ungodliness of which you have been guilty ought to keep you back from the hope of grace. Yet, so that you do not put all works aside and sit down in idle inactivity, so that you do not go on in sin while relying upon grace, remember this: as soon as the desire for grace awakens within you, if it is sincere, it will be manifest in the doing of God's will.

We will be able to pray with confidence and in truth, *"Forgive us our debts,"* only when we just as heartily attempt to say, *"As we forgive our debtors"* (Matt. 6:12). Similarly, John wrote,

> Let us not love in word, neither in tongue; but in deed and in truth. And hereby we know that we are of the truth, and shall assure our hearts before him....If our heart condemn us not, then have we confidence toward God. (1 John 3:18–19)

In this manner, we learn to correctly understand the Scripture, *"Work...for it is God which worketh in you"* (Phil. 2:12–13). He works in us by faith, and our works become the lovely evidence of His heavenly grace, the belief in His everlasting favor.

Chapter 11

Faith That Glorifies God

He staggered not at the promise of
God through unbelief; but was strong
in faith, giving glory to God...Therefore
it was imputed to him for righteousness.
— Romans 4:20, 22

Those who have not yet come to faith and who do not yet fully understand it often ask, "Why is faith so highly regarded by the Lord and capable of such great things?" The answer is simple: faith gives glory to God. It humbles the sinner in the dust and causes him to realize that he is one who deserves nothing and is capable of nothing. On this account, he must present himself to God as dependent on the promises of a free compassion.

Faith glorifies God because it acknowledges His power and love through which redemption is bestowed. It glorifies His Word and faithfulness, too, since these are so strong and glorious that the sinner can commit himself to them, though he has nothing else. Faith sets God and man in the right relationship to one another—God on the throne of His sovereign grace, from whom everything must and will come; man in his misery and nothingness, as one who has nothing in himself but guilt and its curse.

In the other virtues of the Christian life, such as humility and love, there is always something that is worked in man. He can feel it, and he might even boast about it. True faith, on the other hand, is the confession of utter poverty and helplessness. It says, "I have nothing left; I can do nothing. I must now simply remain silent to hear what God speaks, to see what He will do, to receive what He will give."

Faith truly has a beggar's attitude, by which man is laid in the dust. And yet, no angel in heaven can give God as much honor as faith does, for out of the surrounding darkness and sin and poverty, faith still relies on God and expects from Him the certain fulfillment of that which He has promised.

THERE IS NO GLORY IN UNBELIEF

Oh, how great is the foolishness of the heart of man! So many people actually imagine that they give glory to God by their unbelief. They imagine that they honor God when they mourn excessively over themselves and their misery, when they say how unworthy they are to take hold of such grace because they have such a deep sense of the greatness and holiness of God. On the contrary, it is really to His dishonor. They make it seem as if He were not sufficiently gracious toward the unworthy, not sufficiently powerful to rescue the utterly wretched, not absolutely faithful to perform His Word.

Faith alone gives glory to God, for it sets no limits on the Holy One of Israel. It has but one question:

what has God said? Once it knows the answer to this, then it asks nothing further about possibility or truth or anything else. The Word of God is enough for faith. Like Abraham, we may give glory to God by being strong in faith.

Beloved reader, it is a terrible sin to rob God of His honor. By not believing, you make yourself guilty of this offense. As God has revealed Himself in the Gospel more gloriously than in the Law, so the sin of unbelief in relation to the promises is much more dreadful than that of disobedience to the commandments. For this reason, I entreat you, believe what God says. Do not ask what you are or what you have, but ask if there is anything that God would have you now believe or if there is any promise with which He comes to meet the ungodly. Here is one: *"Christ died for the ungodly"* (Rom. 5:6). Receive that word, keep it in your heart, ponder and believe it, and do not rest until it abides as an essential truth within you, even as it is with God.

Christ is for the ungodly. Yes, this very day, your soul ought to give glory to the Lord by going to Him as the gracious, almighty, and faithful Redeemer. Anxious one, why do you not believe? This is the only thing that you are to do, the only thing that God will have: *"Only believe"* (Mark 5:36). Commit yourself to His Word, be strong in faith, and through this give glory to God as you go to Him.

HAVING FAITH IN HIS PROMISES

A simple and understandable example of faith that brings glory to God is found in the story of Sarah. *"Through faith also Sara[h] herself received strength...because she judged him faithful who had promised"* (Heb. 11:11). By believing in His promises, she brought glory to His name.

There was a time when Sarah doubted. She looked to nature and believed that she could no longer bear children. Through the repeated promises of the Lord, she was nevertheless led to look to Him who had given those promises. Keeping in mind His divine faithfulness, she found there was no alternative for her but to believe. And, the only account that she could give of the supernatural expectation of faith was this: *"He is faithful that promised"* (Heb. 10:23).

The same course must be followed today by Christians who desire to be liberated from their doubts and to reach the blessed experiences of the life of faith. We must learn to disregard the reasonings of the mind. The questions that nature would have asked first, such as "How can these things be?" and "How will I know that it is so?" must no longer be asked. All our calculations are invalid when we try to determine whether our own wisdom and power can bring us to where we know we must be. We must make ourselves content with the view expressed in this sentence: *"He is faithful that promised."*

The only thing that one has to ask is this: "Is there also a promise for me?" If the Word of God gives us the answer—*"This is a faithful saying, and worthy of all acceptation, that Christ Jesus came into the world to save sinners; of whom I am chief"* (1 Tim. 1:15)—then that is sufficient to bring us down before the Lord. It is enough to make us expect that He will perform the promise to us: *"He is faithful that promised"* (Heb. 10:23).

Faith That Glorifies God

GOD IS FAITHFUL

Oh, if you would only keep yourself occupied with the consideration of God's faithfulness, how your unbelief would be ashamed! When anxious feelings multiply in you, and you fear for yourself and your work, go and bow down in silent meditation and adoration before your God as the Faithful One. Then, your whole spirit will become filled with the thoughts and the peace that spring up from this state. Go over all the assurances in the Scriptures, so glorious and clear. The Unchangeable One Himself will fulfill His promises.

All that God desires of us is the stillness that observes and expects His performance. Consult the believers of the old and new covenants, reflect on their ways and their leadings, and they will tell you with one accord that the one source of their strength and their peace has been the faithfulness of God.

Therefore, familiarize yourself every day with every promise of God that you read. Pray every day to receive what God has spoken to you. Look to see that you will indeed be a partaker of the offered salvation. Accustom yourself to focusing undividedly on the Word, to letting your whole heart be filled with it: *"He is faithful that promised"* (Heb. 10:23). And, above all, even when you are not yet able to take hold of everything, do not forget to praise and to thank God for His faithfulness. Praise and adore Him as the Faithful One. Your adoration will confirm your faith in Him and will bring glory to Him.

You must not set your hope on the divine faithfulness only when you are taking the first steps on the path of conversion or only when you are seeking forgiveness and acceptance. Rather, you must trust in divine faithfulness throughout the struggle. In this way, you will make it your habit to trust in Him until the end, so that you may be found unworthy of rebuke in the Day of our Lord Jesus.

It was when his whole focus was set on this hope that Paul said, *"God is faithful, by whom ye were called unto the fellowship of his Son Jesus Christ our Lord"* (1 Cor. 1:9). And, when he wrote, *"The very God of peace sanctify you wholly,"* he immediately added, *"Faithful is he that calleth you, who also will do it"* (1 Thess. 5:23–24). It is a wonder to me that so little belief in that glorious work of sanctification is found today.

It was by this faith, this loyal regard for the faithfulness of her God and reliance upon it, that Sarah received the capacity to bear a child. This kind of faith does not lead to sluggishness and indifference; instead, it increases activity. Faith teaches the believer to wait upon God spiritually and earnestly, so that He may point out to him what he must do. And, God demonstrates that a person may learn by experience to understand the deep significance of the following verses: *"Work...for it is God which worketh in you"* (Phil. 2:12–13). Believing in God's faithfulness to work in him, the believer then has courage to work for God. *"Through faith also Sara[h] herself received strength...because she judged him faithful who had promised"* (Heb. 11:11).

BELIEVING AND RECEIVING

You can only receive such a strong faith that glorifies God when you have believed in and received

Faith That Glorifies God

Jesus. *"As many as received him, to them gave he power to become the sons of God, even to them that believe on his name"* (John 1:12). From this verse, you may conclude that receiving the Lord Jesus is the same as believing on His name. One receives Him as soon as one believes on His name. His name is always Jesus, Savior. As soon as you believe this and look on Him as the Man who certainly saves the sinner, you will not think, "He can do this, but I do not know if He will do this in me." Instead, you will regard Him as the Savior given by God also for you, and thus you will believe on His name. You will believe that His name essentially expresses what Jesus is.

As soon as you do this, you receive Him and bring glory to Him. You, as a sinner, acknowledge Him in His grace as Jesus; you take hold of Him in the faith that says, "He is also for me." You receive Him as a gift bestowed by God, set before Him to be claimed by every sinner. You therefore receive Him as what His name signifies—Savior, the one and only perfect Savior.

BECOMING A CHILD OF GOD

The sinner acknowledges that there is not and never will be anything good in himself. He foresees much unfaithfulness and backsliding on his own part. He feels himself to be wholly powerless. However, he receives Jesus as a Savior, as one who undertakes the whole work, who from day to day will continue that work and accomplish it in the leading, the keeping, and the sanctification of the soul. And, the more he believes in that name—in the absolute truth, the far-reaching significance, the inexhaustible power of that name—the more perfectly he will receive Jesus in the riches of His many blessings. At that point, he experiences the truth, that Jesus saves.

Christ gives power to men to become the sons of God. He enables them also to say, through the Spirit, "Abba, Father." With all the dispositions of children—confidence, fear, love, obedience—they are to rejoice in God's fatherly love.

Reader, are you seeking salvation? Oh, then, receive Jesus. God offers Him to you as a Savior. Receive Him as a gift of the divine love. Acknowledge that He is intended for you. Believe that, with His name, the work of saving a sinner may well be entrusted to Him. Receive Him in that faith, coupled with the simple surrender of yourself, dead and wretched as you are, and be assured that you will not come out deceived.

Push away all doubts! I must be straightforward with you because we are dealing with your salvation, so I ask you: do you believe in the name of Jesus, or do you not believe in it? Do you believe in the name Jesus, given by the true God to His Son so that you may build your hope upon it?

O sinner, believe that the name of Jesus is divine truth. Say today, "Yes, He is the Savior of that which was lost." No longer shut Him out, but receive Him in your heart with simple faith in His name, Jesus. Begin with this, continue with this, go forward with this, and believe even more in the name Jesus. Receive Him with this, and He will give you power to become a child of God.

I must tell you once more what God says to you today, and thousands on earth and in heaven can confirm that it is really so: *"As many as received him, to them gave he power to become the sons of God, even to them that believe on his name"* (John 1:12). Through your faith in Him and His promises, you will bring glory to His name.

Chapter 12

Expressions
of Faith

Then believed they his words;
they sang his praise.
—Psalm 106:12

Your salvation comes through faith when you
believe on the name of Jesus. That, I hope, has been
made clear to you. Through faith and the confession
of your sins, you are forgiven of sins and cleansed
from unrighteousness (1 John 1:9). This forgiveness
ought to be cause for rejoicing and thanksgiving.

A DESCRIPTION OF FORGIVENESS

Let us look more closely at this forgiveness, first
by describing it. Then I will show how thanksgiving
should arise from the faith that has been given to
you.

A Simple Meaning

God's forgiveness is, first of all, very simple. The
meaning of this verse is simple enough that everyone

can understand it. Everyone knows what is meant when an earthly father forgives his child. He tells him that he will no longer remember his sins, will not blame him for the harm that was done, and will not punish him. He will deal with the child as if he had done no harm at all.

In the same way, the guilty and condemned sinner looks to God on high and says, "Lord, with You there is forgiveness. My guilt is heavy. I have deserved Your severest punishment, but with You there is forgiveness. You, in your grace, have promised to acquit the guilty of everything and not to impute his sins to him." Because the sinner is exposed to the curse and can do nothing of himself to contribute to salvation, this is the simple and, at the same time, the only way by which he can be saved. The divine acquittal from all guilt is received without the least worthiness or merit on his part, and entirely without cost.

Glorious Assurance

God's forgiveness of your sins is not only simple, but it is also glorious. Should not everyone desire this blessing? When David cried unto God, he said, *"If thou, LORD, shouldest mark iniquities, O Lord, who shall stand?"* (Ps. 130:3). Anyone who cries *"out of the depths"* (v. 1), as David did, will find that it is glorious to be able to look up to God with the assurance that He will blot out all these sins and bring them to nothing. Indeed, it is very blessed to look up to God out of distress and anxiety, out of heavy guilt and deep misery, and to say: *"'There is forgiveness with thee'* (v. 4). The Lord looks upon me in grace.

Expressions of Faith

His anger is turned away from me, and He comforts me."

What a blessed peace, what a heavenly joy then falls on the heart! It is indeed glorious, in the face of all conviction of sin and experience of misery, in the face of every thought of death and judgment, to be able to say, *"There is forgiveness with thee."* Who would not desire it?

Absolute Certainty

God's forgiveness is also so sure that everyone may believe it. The whole Bible announces that our forgiveness lies with God. Jesus came from heaven to obtain and to seal it for us. His blood is the pledge of it. Thousands of the greatest sinners can support the truth of the cry, "There is forgiveness with God." All heaven confirms it. Eternity will echo it: "There is forgiveness with God." It is sure.

The certainty of it does not depend on your faith. Whether you believe it or not, whether you despise it or not, there is forgiveness with God. As truly as He is God, He is a God of forgiveness, a God who abundantly pardons. As certain as you are that He is God, you may you be certain that there is forgiveness with Him. Even before you believe it, it is truth, and you may rest your soul and safely commit yourself to God upon it. You will experience it, for with God there is sure forgiveness.

Powerful Blessings

Furthermore, God's forgiveness is so powerful that everyone can receive blessing from it. Although you have no faith as of yet, take this word as a living seed into your heart, and it will awaken faith. Although you do not yet dare to call God your Father, set His Word in your heart, give it a place there, think it over, and say aloud before your God, "Lord, *there is forgiveness with thee'* (Ps. 130:4)."

This word is living and powerful; it will cause hope to rise in your soul. It will inspire you with new thoughts about God, and it will instill into you confidence and boldness before Him. Without knowing it, you will begin to say: *"There is forgiveness with thee'* for me, too." It will awaken the fear and love of God in your soul. It will bind you to Jesus. It will cause you to dedicate yourself wholly to Him.

Poor, sinful soul, do not mourn any longer over your weakness. Receive these words of confidence; they are living and powerful. Go with them trustfully to your knees, and, although it may be the thousandth time, use them as the language of your heart to God: "Lord, *there is forgiveness with thee.'"* This language will work mightily, and faith and peace and love will be its fruits.

Beloved reader, I offer to you these words from God. God gives you freedom to use these words with Him. God commands you to think of Him in this manner. Your may say in your heart, "I do not know for sure that I can find forgiveness with God." In that case, let go of these perverse thoughts of yours, and make room for God's thoughts in your soul.

Stand firmly in the thought, "There is forgiveness with God," and you will soon be able to add, "Also for me." Moreover, you will soon learn to sing, *"Bless the LORD, O my soul,...who forgiveth all thine iniquities"* (Ps. 103:2–3). Your faith will be expressed in singing God's praises. *"Then believed they his words; they sang his praise."*

THANKSGIVING AND FAITH

Once you know that you have been forgiven, will you not want to thank the One who has forgiven you? Will you not believe in His name even more? Where faith is active and growing, it will always be coupled with thanksgiving. This is another expression of our faith in God.

The apostle expressed this in Colossians 2:7: *"Rooted and built up in him, and stablished in the faith,...abounding therein with thanksgiving."* Faith stirs one to thanksgiving, which in turn strengthens faith. The psalmist wrote, *"Then believed they his words; they sang his praise."* Faith and thanksgiving belong to one another and keep one another. The more I believe, the more I will thank; the more I thank, the more I will believe.

The lack of faith is the reason why men so rarely offer thanks. Likewise, the neglect of thanksgiving hinders and weakens faith. This is a fault to which too little attention has been paid and from which many people suffer great loss. Let us consider it for a moment.

ENTIRELY OCCUPIED WITH GOD

The reason why thanksgiving has the effect of increasing faith is rather obvious. Faith has its greatest power in the fact that, in believing, the sinner wholly forgets himself and looks to God. With undivided energy, he hears God and goes out wholly to Him. And this is precisely the nature of thanksgiving.

In thanksgiving, the soul must be entirely occupied with God, with the contemplation of His goodness, the adoration of His Godhead, the consideration of His ways, and the expression of His wonders. Accordingly, the more the mind is exercised in this work and is taken up with the thought of all this, the more the mind will be convinced that the Lord is truly a God on whom it is meant to rely. If thanksgiving—which is the express mention of His omnipotence, His love, His faithfulness, and His perfection—fills a man's heart, the result must be that the man earnestly desires to concentrate on God. If he has only a single word from such a God upon which to build his faith, he has enough.

In such thanksgiving, a man will have his desire awakened, his courage strengthened, and his inward devotion to God deepened. The shamefulness of his unbelief will be very manifest as an offense against such a God. The remembrance of unbelief, of his unworthiness, his lack of love, his insincerity, his weakness, and his uncertainty as to whether he will remain faithful—all this will be utterly blotted out by what the thankful heart has expressed. That is, that God in His compassionate and omnipotent love is greater than all the forces of sin and Satan. It cannot be otherwise if thanksgiving increases faith. That is why the Scriptures say, *"Abounding therein with thanksgiving"* (Col. 2:7).

And on the other hand, you who are seeking the increase of faith, are you thanking God? If you are still unconverted, go and thank Him that you are still not in hell. Oh, what a wonder it is that, in His longsuffering, He has still borne with you and spared you. Thank Him for this. Thank Him that He gave His Son Jesus for sinners. Yes, although you are not yet able to say that He is yours, fall upon your knees and thank God for His unspeakable gift to this sinful world and also to you. Thank Him for His gracious promise that has also come to you.

LET YOUR PRAISES BE HEARD

O sinner, though you have as yet received little or nothing for yourself, do not be silent. Instead, adore and speak of His wonderful compassion. Let this be your daily task. Keep yourself intensely occupied with it. Let your soul abide in contemplating who God is, what He has done, what He has promised to do, how gracious, how faithful He is, and how mighty to deliver.

Therefore, endeavor to express this on your knees before Him, however imperfect your words appear. In every acknowledgment of your bitter misery, thank Him that He is God; confess before Him that He is great and good.

This thanksgiving will teach you that you may calmly confide in God. And, throughout the whole conflict of faith, you will often be able to say that, when everything looked utterly dark and your wretchedness was very deep, hope was once more revived in your heart when you simply offered thanks for who and what God is. Whatever else fails you, this always remains—a God to praise.

Your case was never so wretched that you had nothing left to be thankful for. Just put this remedy to the test: in the midst of all that is dark, grievous, and incomprehensible for the soul, only begin to praise, and your praising will quickly merge into believing. Praising and believing will be one in you, and your faith will find expression in all that you do.